YORK NOTES

General Editors: Professor A.N. Jeffar [
of Stirling) & Professor Suheil Bushru
University of Beirut)

Harper Lee

TO KILL A MOCKINGBIRD

Notes by Rosamund Metcalf

MA B LITT (OXFORD)
Lecturer, Department of English,
University of Swaziland

LONGMAN
YORK PRESS

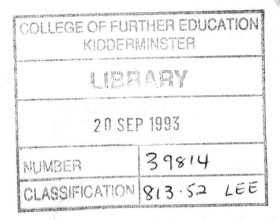
YORK PRESS
Immeuble Esseily, Place Riad Solh, Beirut.

LONGMAN GROUP LIMITED
Longman House, Burnt Mill, Harlow,
Essex CM20 2JE, England
and Associated companies throughout the world

© Librairie du Liban 1981

First published 1981
Reprinted 1982, 1984 and 1985
ISBN 0 582 78201 5
Produced by Longman Group (FE) Ltd
Printed in Hong Kong

Contents

Part 1

Introduction

The author

Harper Lee belongs to the younger generation of writers from the American South which has emerged since the Second World War. She was born in 1926 in Monroeville, Alabama, a small Southern town closely resembling Maycomb, where the novel is set, both in its geographical location near the town of Montgomery and in its general character. Like Scout, who is the narrator of the novel, Harper Lee was educated at local public schools. Later she went on to the Alabama State University. The novel may be said, therefore, to be firmly based in the author's own background experience. It came out in 1960, won the momentous Pulitzer prize, and soon afterwards was made into a film starring Gregory Peck in the role of Atticus Finch. The author now lives in New York. She has not yet produced any further novels.

General historical background

Some knowledge of the history of the American South, and of the Civil War of 1861–5 in particular, is essential to a proper understanding of *To Kill a Mockingbird*. The novel is actually set in the period from 1933 to 1935, but the past is still strongly alive in the minds of the characters, and the moral and social issues with which the novel is concerned are those which were fought over in the Civil War. Study of the novel's historical background should begin, therefore, with that conflict.

The bond between the states in the American Union was always fragile. From the time when the original thirteen colonies declared their independence from Britain in 1776 there was always the possibility that individual states would break away from the group. In the event, however, they stayed together until divided by the issue of slavery which in 1861 split the South from the North. Some cultural differences between the South and the North had always existed. The South was an agricultural society, deriving its wealth from the production of cotton, tobacco, rice, sugar and hemp on plantations worked by black slaves, descendants of the Africans imported into the United States from the seventeenth century onwards through the slave trade. The Northern states had a more urban, industrialised economy, and as time passed

Northerners became more and more unwilling to condone what they felt to be the evil of slavery in the South. Southerners justified their practice by arguing that the black race was naturally inferior, and that the imported Africans were actually fortunate to be American slaves, since their slavery brought them into contact with Christianity and civilisation. At times the slave system was enforced with great brutality, and at best Southern whites tended to regard their black slaves as ignorant, simple-minded, child-like, lazy, irresponsible and in need of firm guidance from their white superiors. This attitude may still be observed among the white inhabitants of Maycomb County in *To Kill a Mockingbird*.

The division between North and South came to a crisis in 1861, when the Southern states of Virginia, North Carolina, South Carolina, Georgia, Alabama, Tennessee, Louisiana, Arkansas, Mississippi, Florida, and Texas broke away from the Union, joined themselves together as the Confederate States of America, and went to war with the rest of the country. Both sides expected a short war. At the start President Lincoln called for volunteers for the Union side to join up for three months only. Fighting dragged on, however, till 1865, when General Robert E. Lee, on behalf of the Southern Confederacy, surrendered to the Northern Union General Ulysses Grant.

The suffering on both sides had been terrible, and the South was unable to forget. The bitterness of their defeat was then exacerbated by the reconstruction period which followed, when the new Northern rulers attempted to reshape Southern society and to give practical force to the emancipation of the blacks, by offering them political power. For the white Southerners the whole experience of defeat and reconstruction only served to strengthen their sense of separate identity and their loyalty to distinctive Southern values and traditions. They continued to give their children the names of Confederate Generals (several examples of this practice can be found in *To Kill a Mockingbird*), and they refused to change their attitude to the newly emancipated blacks. The poor whites, in particular, who had never owned slaves in the pre-war period, now greatly feared and resented the free blacks, whom they saw as a threat to their own security and status. During the reconstruction period white Southerners successfully resisted government efforts to implement ideas of social and political equality for blacks, and many state laws were passed in the South with the object of preserving white supremacy. Similarly, though the rich leisurely life-style of the Old South had been largely destroyed by the Civil War, Southerners continued to pride themselves on the aristocratic elegance of their traditions. All these Southern tendencies can be found in *To Kill a Mockingbird*, where racial prejudice, social snobbery and attachment to 'Southern' values are major motive forces in the plot.

In spite of all that has been said, the novel is not a simple attack on white Southern culture. Harper Lee is indignant about the cruel treatment received by black Americans, but she continues to feel a nostalgic affection for some aspects of the White Southern tradition. In the novel Atticus Finch warns his children not to reject their own community, whatever faults they may find in it. Similarly, Harper Lee criticises Alabama society, but retains some attachment to it.

Literary background

As a writer Harper Lee belongs by birth to a special tradition, that of the Southern novelist. In this century the South has produced a remarkable number of successful authors, of whom the novelist William Faulkner (1897–1962) is probably the most famous. His example quickly inspired others, until by the mid-twentieth century Carson McCullers (1917–67), another Southern novelist, could claim that 'the South at the present time boils with literary energy'. This burst of literary creativity is believed by Southerners to be a result of their defeat in the Civil War, which they feel deepened their sense of tragedy. Whatever the reason, modern Southern writers have produced many novels of high quality and distinctive character. *To Kill a Mockingbird* is a typical Southern novel in that it shares in this distinctive character.

One of the most striking features of Southern novels is their strong regional sense. Defeat in the Civil War only strengthened feelings of local loyalty among Southerners. They had always been deeply attached to their own land, and the isolation of Southern rural communities after the Civil War served to increase the attachment. This has produced valuable results in Southern fiction. As Carson McCullers points out, all novelists tend to write well about environments known in childhood, but Southerners seem to feel with special intensity about their early surroundings. Flannery O'Connor (1925–64), another modern Southern novelist, believes this is a major advantage. 'The best American fiction,' she says, 'has always been regional. The ascendancy passed roughly from New England to the Midwest to the South, it has passed to and stayed longest wherever there has been a shared past, a sense of alikeness, and a possibility of reading a small history in a universal light'. All the qualities listed here can be found in *To Kill a Mockingbird*, in which Maycomb County is described in loving detail, the sense of community is very powerful, and the small local events are shown to be relevant to universal moral issues of justice and equality.

Mention of the importance of the community leads on to another characteristic feature of Southern novels: the powerful evocation of loneliness. Two factors are operating here: the isolation of the South itself and the particular experience of modern Southern writers. In the years of decline after the Civil War the South was largely cut off from the rest of the country. While the rest of the United States was booming, the South was neglected and stagnating, and because of this modern Southern writers are born to some knowledge of social isolation. Secondly, these modern writers themselves often undergo the painful experience of alienation from their own communities. After growing up in their beloved Southern environment almost all of them move away to the North either to complete their education or to work. Upon returning to their homeland they tend to find themselves no longer at home, as they have lost sympathy with Southern values, especially as regards race. They therefore find themselves torn between love and hate for their old community, a community which they know is dying but which they cannot wholeheartedly mourn. All this may help to explain why Southern writers lay such emphasis on and describe so poignantly the pain of not belonging. Harper Lee conforms to the typical pattern; she grew up in a small Southern community and left it for New York. In *To Kill a Mockingbird* the theme of loneliness is repeatedly stressed: loneliness caused by lack of a warm family life, as in the case of Arthur Radley and Dill; the loneliness of growing up, which Scout experiences when she finds her relationship with her brother changing; the loneliness of being social outcasts, as are Mayella Ewell and her family; and the loneliness which arises from racial intolerance, most clearly seen in the reference to Mr Dolphus Raymond's half-caste children, who 'don't belong anywhere'.

The very existence of the black community in the South provides another major common theme for Southern novelists. Though they may feel pride in their gracious aristocratic past Southerners can never escape from the curse and sin of slavery. This produces a sense of guilt which hangs over modern Southern fiction. The evil of slavery cannot be forgotten, since the black Americans are still a visible presence in the South and are still exposed to white intolerance and prejudice. Race relations naturally tend, therefore, to be a central theme in Southern fiction, so the fact that the climactic event of *To Kill a Mockingbird* is the trial and wrongful conviction of a black man places it right in the mainstream of the Southern tradition.

One further characteristic feature of modern Southern fiction is the emphasis on violence, which has been a constant feature from Faulkner onwards. Carson McCullers claims that Southern literature closely resembles classic nineteenth-century Russian fiction, in that both emerge from societies whose dominant characteristic is the cheapness of human life. This is not merely a question of black life, as white Southerners have also traditionally been quick to turn their violence against each other. An instance of this in *To Kill a Mockingbird* is to be found in the account of Atticus Finch's first legal case, in which he defended two men who murdered the local blacksmith in a minor dispute over a horse. Hot temper and swift recourse to violence were always matters of pride in the white Southern tradition, and after the Civil War much of the violence was inevitably directed against the blacks. Moreover, this racial violence became involved with an obscure fear or envy of the black man's sexuality. Thus the classic case of violence in Southern fiction concerns rape followed by lynching and involving a confrontation between black and white. *To Kill a Mockingbird* conforms closely to this pattern: the black Tom Robinson is accused of raping the white Mayella Ewell; a lynching party comes to the jail to get him, and finally, though an innocent man, he dies with seventeen bullet-holes in him. At the end of the novel two children narrowly escape violent death. Harper Lee clearly disapproves of violence, but it is a prominent feature of her description of small-town Southern life in the 1930s.

Finally, Harper Lee's identity as a woman puts her in a special category of Southern writers. Among the successful modern Southern novelists a high proportion have been women. The reasons for this are not clear, though it has been suggested that Southern culture, with its emphasis on close-knit family and local loyalties, provides a specially favourable environment for female writers. In addition to this, the frustrations of female life may themselves contribute to the excellence of Southern female fiction. Women were much idealised in Southern society, which liked to regard them as pure, delicate, fragile beings, unfit to deal with the coarser realities of life. In theory this meant a high status for women, but in practice many women found it restrictive and oppressive. They were therefore in a good position to understand feelings of frustration and oppression in general, and such feelings were common in the South after the Civil War. Black men were oppressed by white, the South was oppressed by the North: the entire community suffered from a sense of frustration. Women in the South, simply because they were women, were particularly well able to capture and convey such feelings. In *To Kill a Mockingbird* a recurrent theme is Scout's resentment of the gracious, ladylike role which her aunt tries to impose on her. Like the heroines of Carson McCullers' novels *The Member of the Wedding* and *The Heart is a Lonely Hunter* she rejects her feminine name of Jean Louise and prefers to use her unfeminine nickname, 'Scout'. The female point of view, therefore, is significant in bringing out certain aspects of the themes of the novel, especially frustration, social oppression and desire for freedom. The fact that Harper Lee is a woman may thus have been of advantage to her in tackling the subject of Southern society.

A note on the text

To Kill a Mockingbird was first published by Lippincott, Philadelphia, in 1960. Its wide popularity has ensured frequent reprintings since that time.

The text used in preparing this guide is the British paperback edition produced by Pan Books, London in association with Heinemann, London, first published in 1974 and also reprinted many times.

Part 2

Summaries
of TO KILL A MOCKINGBIRD

A general summary

The main event in the novel is the trial of a black man, Tom Robinson, who is accused of raping a white girl, Mayella Ewell. The story begins, however, not in the year of the trial, which is 1935, but two years earlier, in the summer of 1933. The narrator is a little girl, Scout Finch, daughter of Tom Robinson's white defence attorney. In the first part of the book she recounts various incidents in which she, her elder brother Jem and their friend Dill are concerned between 1933 and 1934.

When the novel begins Scout is nearly six, Jem is nearly ten, and their friend Dill, who comes to spend his summer holiday in Maycomb with his aunt, is nearly seven. Their main interest in the early part of the book is in trying to establish communication with a neighbour, Arthur Radley, nicknamed 'Boo', who has been shut up in his house for years and who has the reputation of being a dangerous lunatic. In the first summer, 1933, Jem just summons up enough courage to run and touch the Radley house. Then, at the end of the following school year, Jem and Scout find gifts of chewing-gum and polished coins in a hole in a tree outside the Radley house. When Dill comes back to Maycomb in the summer of 1934 he joins them in a game in which they enact what they believe is the true history of the Radley family: Arthur's involvement with a teenage gang, his punishment by incarceration in the house, and his attack on his father with a pair of scissors some years later.

The children's father, Atticus Finch, sees them playing this game and discourages it. Next Jem and Dill try to push a message on the end of a stick into the Radley house. Atticus catches them, and forbids them to try again. On Dill's last evening in Maycomb the children creep to the Radley house and try to peer in at the window. They see the shadow of a man, and run away. Mr Nathan Radley, Arthur's brother, fires a shot into the garden, claiming that he thought a Negro was stealing his vegetables. In escaping Jem gets his trousers caught on the fence, and when he goes to retrieve them later that night he finds the tear in them has been mended. He realises Arthur has helped him.

During the following school year Jem and Scout find further gifts in the tree: a ball of string; carved soap figures; an old medal and a broken watch on a chain with a knife. Jem is aware that the gifts come from

Arthur, so he writes a letter of thanks, intending to put it in the hole. Before he can do so Mr Nathan Radley, who has also realised what is happening, blocks the hole with cement. The children's next contact with the Radleys occurs during a fire at the house of another neighbour, Miss Maudie. While the children stand outside watching the fire on a cold winter's night, Arthur comes unnoticed out of his house to put a blanket round Scout's shoulders. This is their last contact with him until the very end of the novel, when he emerges to save their lives when they are attacked by Bob Ewell. In this way the Radley adventures, which dominate Part One of the book, come to a climax at the end of Part Two.

Apart from the Radley adventures the major episodes in Part One, in order of occurrence, are Scout's first experience of school; the children's Christmas visit to Aunt Alexandra; the shooting of a rabid dog and the encounter with another neighbour, Mrs Dubose.

In her account of her first day at school Scout describes the children of some of the characters who are to play crucial roles in Part Two of the novel. One is Burris Ewell, the son of the man who accuses Tom Robinson of rape; the other is Walter Cunningham, the son of a poor white farmer who leads a lynch mob to the jail where Tom is held. Both boys closely resemble their fathers in character, so their appearance here helps to prepare us for later events.

The next excitements in Part One, again excluding the Radley adventures, are the children's first sight of snow and the burning of Miss Maudie's house. The Christmas following the fire, Atticus gives the children air-rifles, but warns them never to kill mockingbirds, which do no harm. Christmas itself is spent at the home of Aunt Alexandra. There Scout fights her cousin Francis and is punished for it by her bachelor uncle Jack. The next adventure happens in February, when a rabid dog approaches the Finch house. The family's black cook, Cal, warns the neighbours and summons Atticus, who bravely steps into the road and kills the dog with a single shot. The children now discover that he is the best shot in the county, but rarely uses a gun because he feels his skill gives him an unfair advantage over other living creatures.

By this time Atticus has agreed to take on the defence of Tom Robinson. Though the children do not know the details of the case, they soon discover that their father's action is unpopular with the white community. First one of Scout's classmates criticises Atticus for defending 'niggers'. Scout wants to fight to avenge the insult, but Atticus forbids her. Then her cousin Francis makes the same criticism during the Christmas visit, provoking the fight for which Scout is punished. Finally Jem too gets into trouble because of the Robinson case. Mrs Dubose, who lives in a neighbouring house, shouts abuse at the children's father when they pass her house. Jem breaks her flowers in revenge, is sent by Atticus to apologise, and for a month afterwards has to read aloud in the afternoons to the old lady. Scout goes too, and is puzzled by Mrs Dubose's strange, moody behaviour. A few months later the old lady dies, and Atticus explains that she was very ill and had become a morphine addict. She used the reading sessions as a means of conquering her addiction. He tells the children that they should respect such courage. That is the end of Part One.

Part Two begins in the summer of Tom's trial. Scout is feeling lonely, since Jem is growing away from her, Atticus is out of town, and Dill is not coming for the summer as his divorced mother has remarried. One Sunday Cal takes the children to attend the service in the African church, and when they return home they find Aunt Alexandra waiting for them. She has come to look after the family during the period of the trial. Since she is a snobbish person she fits easily into Maycomb society and annoys the children by her efforts to make them behave conventionally. The next excitement happens one evening when Scout feels something strange under her bed, and she and Jem find Dill hiding there. He has run away from home because he felt his mother and stepfather did not really want him. Atticus arranges for Dill to be allowed to spend the rest of the summer in Maycomb, and the children have a week of enjoyment before what Scout calls the 'nightmare' begins.

The 'nightmare' is Tom Robinson's trial. The tension begins when a group of responsible citizens come on Saturday evening to the Finch house to warn Atticus that they fear violence when Tom is moved to the county jail on the following day. The next night Atticus goes to sit outside the jail to protect Tom. A lynch mob led by Walter Cunningham comes to the jail hoping to seize Tom and execute him before the trial begins. Luckily Jem has a premonition of trouble and takes Scout and Dill downtown to find out what is happening. Scout does not realise that the group of men surrounding her father is different from the friendly group who visited the house the previous night, and she runs forward to greet them. Atticus is afraid, but Scout, by her innocent attempts at friendly conversation, reminds Cunningham that the Finch family has been generous to him. He therefore calls off the mob, and the Finches go home to bed. The next morning the trial begins.

Aunt Alexandra forbids the children to attend the trial, but they go anyway, and sit with the black community in the coloured balcony. They hear evidence from the sheriff, from Bob Ewell, the father of the girl who is supposed to have been raped, from Mayella Ewell herself, and from Tom. The sheriff states that he was summoned one evening to the Ewell house, and heard Bob Ewell accuse Tom of having raped Mayella. Bob Ewell claims to have actually witnessed the rape, and Mayella supports her father's story. In his cross-questioning Atticus establishes several points favourable to Tom. He shows that Bob Ewell's pretended concern for his daughter is false, as he did not even think of calling a doctor to tend her injuries. Atticus also brings out the fact that Mayella's bruises were mainly on the right side of her face. When Tom stands up the children see he is crippled. His left arm is useless, making it most unlikely that he could have beaten Mayella in the manner described. After Atticus has completed his examination of the witnesses the truth is clear. Tom had simply been a kind neighbour to Mayella, often assisting her with household tasks and never demanding payment. On the evening of the supposed rape she made sexual advances to him. He resisted, and while he was doing so Bob Ewell arrived, saw what was happening, and immediately threatened to kill Mayella. Tom, realising the danger of the situation, ran away. It was Bob Ewell, then, who beat Mayella. The truth is so clear that the children understand it at once. As the final cross-examination draws to a close Dill starts crying, because he cannot bear the way the prosecuting attorney speaks to Tom. Scout takes him out of the courtroom, and when they return Atticus is making his final appeal to the jury. Jem is certain his father has won the case, but when the jury return after several hours of deliberation, they declare Tom guilty.

On the following day Miss Maudie tries to explain that, though Atticus was defeated, he has also triumphed, since only he could have made the jury take so long to decide a case of this sort. Bob Ewell realises that he has been discredited, and threatens revenge against Atticus. Atticus himself remains optimistic, believing Tom may be acquitted when his appeal is heard in a higher court. However, during a tea-party given by Aunt Alexandra for the ladies of the Missionary Circle, news comes that Tom is dead, shot when trying to escape from prison.

The holidays end; the children return to school; life seems to be quiet again. But Bob Ewell still wants revenge. He tries to break into Judge Taylor's house; he molests Tom's widow, and finally, on the night of Hallowe'en, when Scout has been performing in the Maycomb Pageant, he follows the children home in the dark and attacks them with a knife. They are saved by Arthur Radley, who kills their attacker. Jem's elbow is broken, but otherwise the children are unhurt. Atticus thinks at first that Jem killed Bob Ewell, but the sheriff explains that Arthur was responsible, and they agree to avoid publicity by reporting the death as accidental. Scout then escorts Arthur home and returns to her house, where Atticus puts her to bed. That is the end of the story.

Detailed summaries

Chapter one

Scout introduces her family to the readers, provides a little historical background to Maycomb society, recounts the first meeting with Dill, and opens her narration of the Radley adventures.

NOTES AND GLOSSARY:

... it really began with Andrew Jackson: Andrew Jackson (1767–1845) was an American General and seventh President of the USA. His campaign against the Creek Indians in 1812 led to a treaty in which they were forced to surrender most of their tribal lands, opening the way for further expansion by white settlers in Alabama. Harper Lee is suggesting here that her society has its roots in racial injustice and violence

Atticus: this name suggests virtuous character, as it echoes that of Cicero's friend and correspondent, Titus Pomponius Atticus (109–132BC), a man noted for his upright behaviour

Being Southerners it was a source of shame ... : one aspect of the Southern tradition was pride in belonging to long-established families. This is compared to the British habit of tracing ancestors present at the Norman Conquest of Britain in 1066

... the persecution of those who called themselves Methodists: desire for religious freedom was a common motive for emigration from Great Britain to America in the seventeenth and eighteenth centuries. The Finch family founder was a member of the Methodist sect founded by John Wesley in the eighteenth century and not accepted by the official Church of England

the disturbance between the North and the South: the Civil War of 1861–5

trot-lines: fishing-lines

jackass: donkey, a common symbol of stupidity

Hoover carts: home-made two-wheeled wooden carts, deriving their name from the years of Depression when Herbert Hoover (1874–1964) was President (1928–32)

... it had nothing to fear but fear itself: a quotation from the inaugural address of President Franklin D. Roosevelt (1884–1945) after his election in November 1932. He succeeded President Hoover

collard: a variety of cabbage popular in the South

Dracula: Dill has seen the 1931 film version starring Bela Lugosi in the role of the bloodsucking vampire

right puny: very puny. 'Right', meaning 'very', is a typical feature of Southern dialect

picture show: film

a pocket Merlin: Merlin was the magician in the Arthurian legends. 'Pocket' here means small-sized

Oliver Optic, Victor Appleton and Edgar Rice Burroughs: three writers of adventure stories for boys. The Tarzan adventures of Burroughs are still popular today

a cold snap: a spell of cold weather

stumphole whisky: whisky illegally distilled. Prohibition, which outlawed alcoholic beverages under Amendment XVIII to the American Constitution, was in force from 1920 to 1933

flivver: a cheap Ford car

. . . Boo would die of cold from the damp: compare this with accounts of Boo's state of health on pages 266 and 274

Chapter two

In September Dill goes home and Scout starts school. She finds it disappointing; her teacher tells her she should not have learned to read and write at home, and she gets into trouble for trying to explain why the teacher should not embarrass Walter Cunningham by offering to lend him money to buy lunch.

NOTES AND GLOSSARY:

I am from North Alabama . . . : when Alabama joined the confederacy in 1861 an unsuccessful attempt was made to form a neutral state in Northern Alabama, where there were few slaves. Miss Caroline is therefore at once suspected of not being a true Southerner. This shows that the Civil War is still very much a live issue in Alabama in 1933

denim-shirted and floursack-skirted: the majority of the first-grade children come from poor rural families. They are accustomed to the harsh realities of life, and so find the sentimental fantasies their teacher reads to them incomprehensible

union suit: a long woollen undergarment, combining vest and pants, with a flap at the back which could be unfastened

the Dewey Decimal System: a system for cataloguing library books. Jem has confused its name with that of an experimental teaching method. The implication may be that the modern method lacks humanity and treats children as if they were inanimate objects like books. Thus Scout is officially classified as a beginner and the fact that she is literate is ignored

Church baskets: baskets of provisions given by church congregations to the poor

scrip stamps: a system of private charity for the poor

entailment: the legal settlement of land on a number of persons in succession, so that it cannot be dealt with by any one possessor as absolute owner

smilax: a sweet-smelling shrub

the crash hit them hardest: the financial collapse of 1929, which caused a worldwide economic depression

a WPA job: the Works Projects Administration was part of the National Recovery Act of 1933. Its purpose was to provide jobs for the unemployed during the Depression

if he held his mouth right: if he behaved in an ingratiating manner towards government officials

---

Chapter three

During the lunch break Jem and Scout invite Walter Cunningham to eat at their house. In school after lunch the teacher has an argument with a rude, dirty boy called Burris Ewell. In the evening Scout asks Atticus to. let her give up school, but he persuades her to continue.

NOTES AND GLOSSARY:

haint: ghost

pizened: poisoned

Miss Priss: a nickname implying demure, conventional, lady-like behaviour. Jem uses it to insult Scout

what the sam hill: a euphemistic version of 'what the hell'

that boy's yo's comp'ny: that boy is your guest

cootie: louse

relief checks: government money provided to support the unemployed during the Depression

last-will-and-testament-diction: formal style and language, like that used in legal documents such as wills

---

Chapter four

Scout continues to be bored at school. One day, as she walks home, she finds some chewing-gum in a hole in a tree outside the Radley house. Later she and Jem find some old polished coins in the same place. Dill arrives for the summer and the children play their Radley drama game until Atticus sees them and shows his displeasure

NOTES AND GLOSSARY:

scuppernongs: a variety of grape indigenous to the South

in a pig's ear: I don't believe you

the Rover boys: a popular series of boys' adventure stories

Yawl hush: 'You all be quiet.' 'You all' is the distinctive second person plural pronoun form used in the South

trod water at the gate hesitated before entering

his worst performance was Gothic: the Gothic Revival in late eighteenth-century England was a wave of sensational melo-dramatic romances

Chapter five

As the summer passes Jem and Dill spend a lot of time playing together, leaving Scout to talk to a neighbour, Miss Maudie. Finally, she discovers they are planning to push a message on a stick into the Radley house. Atticus catches them at it, and scolds them for tormenting Arthur Radley.

NOTES AND GLOSSARY:

a chameleon lady: the chameleon (a lizard-like creature) can change its colour to match its background. Miss Maudie's appearance varies according to her occupation

the Second Battle of the Marne: the last German offensive in the 1914–18 War. The Germans were turned back, as Miss Maudie hopes to turn back the nut-grass

an Old Testament pestilence: the Plagues of Egypt. See the Bible, Exodus, 7–12

trying to get Miss Maudie's goat: trying to annoy her

a foot-washing Baptist: a member of the extreme Protestant Baptist sect who practise washing of each other's feet as a sign of humility, in imitation of Christ's washing of his disciples' feet. See the Bible, John, 13:5

nome: no, ma'am

I was ravelling a thread: I was following a train of thought

could tell the biggest ones: could tell the biggest lies

Brigadier General Joe Wheeler: a Confederate General (1836–1906)

Chapter six

On Dill's last evening in Maycomb the children try to look through the window of the Radley house. They see a shadow, and as they run away through the garden a shot is fired. The neighbours are roused by the noise, and Mr Nathan Radley tells them he was shooting at a thieving Negro in his garden. In climbing the Radley fence Jem loses his trousers, so he has to go back to retrieve them later that night.

NOTES AND GLOSSARY:

Jem whistled bob-white: imitated a bird-call as a signal to Dill

Angel May: another insulting nickname, this time implying sweetness and virtue

the kingdom coming: the end of the world, when it is believed angels will blow trumpets to wake the dead

strip poker: a gambling game in which players pay forfeits in the form of articles of their clothing

cards were fatal: this is an indication of the puritanism of Maycomb society

Chapter seven

School reopens; Jem seems moody and eventually confesses to Scout that when he went back to fetch his trousers he found them mended. The children discover more gifts in the tree and decide to write a letter of thanks. Mr Nathan Radley prevents them from delivering it by blocking the hole with cement. He says he has done so because the tree is sick, but when the children ask Atticus about it he tells them the tree is perfectly healthy.

NOTES AND GLOSSARY:

to walk flat: to imitate the appearance of Egyptians in ancient Egyptian art

hoodooing: putting a curse on someone. In traditional witch-craft this can be done by making a wax model representing the person to be cursed and then piercing it with pins

bangs: a fringe of hair cut across the forehead

Jem walked on eggs: he walked with great care

he has been crying: Jem is crying out of pity for Arthur

Chapter eight

Winter comes to Maycomb County, bringing the first snow the children have ever seen. Jem shows enterprise and imagination in his making of a snowman. Miss Maudie's house burns to the ground that night, and while the children watch the fire a blanket is put round Scout's shoulders by Arthur Radley.

NOTES AND GLOSSARY:

the Rosetta stone: an ancient stone with inscriptions in three languages found in the Nile Delta in 1799. It enabled the French archaeologist Champollion to make the first translations of Egyptian hieroglyphics. Mr Avery uses it as a symbol of unarguable authority

Appomattox: the name of the village where General Lee surrendered to the Northern forces in 1865. This is another example of the dominance of the Civil War in the Southern imagination

a jim-dandy job: a fine job

morphodite: an invented word, derived from the Greek word meaning 'shape'. The implication is that the snowman reproduces exactly the shape of Mr Avery

Squaw-fashion: like an American Indian woman

shoot: never mind

in a jiffy: in a moment

Chapter nine

Atticus has agreed to defend Tom Robinson. One of Scout's classmates tells her that her father is a disgrace; she wants to fight him, but Atticus prevents her. He explains that his conscience compels him to take the case, even though he has no hope of winning. At Christmas at Aunt Alexandra's house Scout's cousin Francis repeats the insult to Atticus. This time Scout fights and wins. Uncle Jack punishes her, but when she tells him the reason for the fight he apologises.

NOTES AND GLOSSARY:

General Hood: a Confederate General (1831–79), famous for his very long beard

the Missouri Compromise: the agreement worked out in Congress in 1820, by which Missouri was accepted into the Union as a slave state, but slavery was prohibited in other parts of the Louisiana territory. This compromise probably delayed the outbreak of the Civil War. Southern conservatives like Cousin Ike Finch deplore the Missouri compromise as the first instance of Southern concession to Northern prejudice against slavery

Stonewall Jackson: a Confederate General (1824–63), nicknamed 'Stonewall' because of his courage at the battle of Bull Run, where he stood like a stone wall in the face of the Union attack

changelings:	children exchanged as babies by fairies, who take the human infant and substitute a fairy child
she was cold and she was there:	a reference to the reply made by the British explorer G.L. Mallory when asked why he wanted to climb Everest: 'because it's there'. Aunt Alexandra resembles Everest in that she is a cold and unalterable fact of nature
Rose Aylmer:	the name of a girl in a love poem by W.S. Landor (1775–1864), in which he ascribes to her 'every virtue, every grace'. Uncle Jack, as a confirmed bachelor, finds female perfection only in a cat
a widow's walk:	a balcony on the roof, on which sailors' wives could walk as they watched the sea for their husbands' return
ambrosia:	a sweet confection of coconut and orange
fuss:	quarrel

a funny near-sighted old gentleman: Dr Samuel Johnson (1709–84), the author and lexicographer

an old Prime Minister: Lord Melbourne (1779–1848)

Let this cup pass from you: Uncle Jack quotes Christ's words on the evening before his execution, when he prayed to be spared if this were in accordance with God's will. See the Bible, Matthew, 26:39. Atticus knows his involvement in the trial will cause suffering for all his family, but his conscience compels him to suffer, like Christ, on behalf of his community

Chapter ten

Atticus is older than the fathers of most of the children's schoolmates, and they feel embarrassed by his failure to engage in manly sports. In February a rabid dog approaches their house, and Atticus kills it with a single shot. The children then learn that he is actually the best shot in the county.

NOTES AND GLOSSARY:

a jew's harp:	a musical instrument consisting of a small iron frame in which a single metal strip vibrates
bird dog:	hunting dog
moseyin' along:	moving slowly
a-list:	leaning sideways

If I had my 'druthers: if I had my preference

Chapter eleven

An old lady, Mrs Dubose, shouts insults at Atticus when the children pass her house. Jem attacks her flowers in revenge, and Atticus makes him apologise and read aloud in the afternoons to Mrs Dubose as a penance. Some time later she dies, and Atticus tells the children she was a drug-addict who suffered great pain but was determined to break her addiction before dying.

NOTES AND GLOSSARY:

a CSA pistol: a Confederate Army pistol
sassiest: sauciest, most impertinent
mutts: stupid persons
playing hooky: playing truant
camisole: old-fashioned female undergarment
philippic: bitter attack. The name is derived from the attacks made on Philip of Macedon by the orator Demosthenes (383–322BC)
guff: nonsense
he had ... a slow fuse: he was not quick to lose his temper
Ivanhoe: a novel by Sir Walter Scott (1771–1832), very suitable in this context as it concerns the chivalric world of medieval England. Jem, reading aloud to Mrs Dubose, is learning to be a chivalrous gentleman in the modern manner

Chapter twelve

Dill is not to come to Maycomb for the summer, since his mother has remarried. Atticus has to go to Montgomery to work for the state legislature. While he is away Cal takes the children to a service at the black church. On returning home they find Aunt Alexandra there.

NOTES AND GLOSSARY:

Shadrach: one of three persons thrown into a furnace by King Nebuchadnezzar as a punishment for refusing to worship his golden idol. See the Bible, Daniel, 1:7
Mardi Gras: the festival held the day before the beginning of Lent, the period of fasting and abstinence in the Christian calendar
Jubilee: a favourite hymn among black Christians, since its references to crossing the river of death to a heavenly reward could be interpreted as referring to emancipation from slavery

bootleggers: suppliers of illegal alcohol

a spite fence: a fence deliberately built to keep neighbours out

papoose-style: like American Indian babies

Blackstone's Commentaries: a popular exposition of English law, written by Sir William Blackstone (1723–80)

puttin' on airs to beat Moses: behaving arrogantly. Moses was a favourite biblical hero among black Americans, since he led the Israelites out of bondage in Egypt

Enamoured: the word is here intended to mean 'wearing armour'. Aunt Alexandra has stiff corsets

Chapter thirteen

Atticus explains that Aunt Alexandra has come to stay for the summer. She antagonises the children at once by her snobbish and conventional attitudes.

NOTES AND GLOSSARY:

shinny: alcohol made from corn

Rice Christians: Asian Christians who professed conversion to Christianity in order to obtain the supplies of rice handed out by missionaries

born in the objective case: always criticising others

Reconstruction rule: the government of the South in the post-Civil-War period

mandrake roots: mandrakes are plants whose roots resemble human babies, and are reputed to scream when pulled out of the ground. Scout is seeking a supernatural origin for Aunt Alexandra, since it is hard to believe she is a natural sister of Atticus and Jack

he went round the bend: he went crazy

Chapter fourteen

Aunt Alexandra begins to annoy Atticus as well as the children. On the night of a family quarrel Scout finds Dill hiding under her bed. He has run away from home because he felt his mother and stepfather did not really love him.

NOTES AND GLOSSARY:

my feathers rose: I became angry. The metaphor is taken from the action of a cock when preparing to fight

Chapter fifteen

Dill gets permission to stay in Maycomb for the rest of the summer. A week later Tom's trial is due to begin. On the weekend before the trial a group of friends comes to warn Atticus that they fear trouble when Tom is brought to the local jail. Atticus makes light of their fears, but goes down to the jail on the following evening to protect Tom. The children follow him, and arrive just in time to save him from a lynch mob led by Walter Cunningham.

NOTES AND GLOSSARY:

that old Sarum bunch: the poor white Cunningham family (see pp.15–16)

Henry W. Grady: a famous journalist and apologist for racialism in the post-Civil-War South

Ku Klux Klan: this was, and is, a secret society of whites noted for its terror tactics. It was founded in the South after the Civil War to campaign against the recently emancipated blacks and to oppose Reconstruction. It was revived during the 1914–18 War with the object of promoting white supremacy and 'pure Americanism'. Its enemies were all those who did not belong to the dominant white Protestant group—Roman Catholics, Jews and blacks. Members concealed their identity by wearing white sheets and hoods. In the early 1920s the Klan was a powerful political force, but it lost influence after the elections of 1926. This is why Atticus says it has gone

a miniature Gothic joke: built in the elaborate Gothic style of architecture, unsuitable for a small building

you're damn tootin': you're certainly right

Chapter sixteen

The trial begins. Atticus and Aunt Alexandra forbid the children to go downtown, and they spend the morning watching the crowds of spectators arriving. In the afternoon they go to the courtroom in spite of their orders, and sit in the coloured balcony with the black people.

NOTES AND GLOSSARY:

Braxton Bragg: a Confederate General (1817–76), said to be the most unpopular general on either side in the Civil War. He suffered from chronic indigestion and bad temper

Mennonites: a strict Christian sect founded in Switzerland in 1523. Its members emigrated to America to escape religious persecution. Mennonites accept no authority except the Bible, and the more extreme among them are opposed to anything 'modern', that is, unsanctioned by the Bible. Buttons and shaving came into this category

a Roman carnival: a cruel spectacle, like the ancient Roman circuses in which men were devoured by wild beasts

William Jennings Bryan: a Democratic candidate for the Presidency in 1896, famed for his oratory and widely popular in the South

children popped the whip: a game in which a line of children hold on to each other while running, and make sudden turns in order to throw off the end child

Nehi Cola: a cheap imitation of Coca Cola

Arlington: Arlington House, which originally belonged to George Washington. It is considered one of the finest examples of American colonial architecture

Atticus aims to defend him: Atticus intends to take his task seriously, and this shocks the old men who feel he is betraying the white community

their stamping ground: their habitual place of resort

champertous connivance: the illegal proceeding whereby a person not otherwise concerned in a law-suit engages to help one of the litigants to prosecute it, on condition that, in the event of success, he is to receive a share of the property in dispute

---

Chapter seventeen

The prosecuting attorney calls two witnesses: the sheriff and Bob Ewell. The sheriff reports that he was called to the Ewell house in November to hear an accusation of rape. Bob Ewell says that he saw the rape taking place. In his cross-examination Atticus casts doubt on Bob Ewell's testimony.

NOTES AND GLOSSARY:

if he took advantage of her: if he raped her

Robert E. Lee Ewell: Robert E. Lee (1807–70) was the most highly respected of all the Confederate Generals. He was himself opposed to slavery, but fought for the South out of loyalty to his home

crepey: crinkled

ruttin':   having sexual intercourse. The word is normally used only of animals

countin' his chickens: a reference to the proverb 'don't count your chickens before they're hatched', that is, 'don't be over-confident'

Chapter eighteen

The prosecuting attorney calls his third witness, Mayella Ewell. She confirms her father's evidence, but again Atticus succeeds in casting doubt on her credibility.

NOTES AND GLOSSARY:

seb'm: seven

Mr Jingle: a character in *Pickwick Papers* (1836) by Charles Dickens (1812–70). Jingle speaks in an abbreviated style, without complete grammatical sentences

dandy: fine

tollable: tolerable

cotton gin: machine used to separate the lint (raw cotton) from the seed

the proof of the pudding: a reference to the proverb 'the proof of the pudding is in the eating', meaning that one should judge by practical experience

Chapter nineteen

Atticus calls his only witness, Tom. Tom testifies that Mayella asked him to help her mend a door, and then made sexual advances to him. He resisted, and ran away when her father arrived. During the prosecuting cross-examination Dill starts crying and Scout takes him out.

NOTES AND GLOSSARY:

totin':   carrying

Maycomb gave them ... the back of its hand: Maycomb did not offer them any friendship

a slap year: a whole year

She says what her papa do to her don't count: there seems to be a hint here that Bob Ewell has himself sexually abused his daughter

ex cathedra **remarks:** remarks made in an official capacity

a big buck: a big male

I didn't go to be: I didn't intend to be

thin-hided: over-sensitive

Chapter twenty

Outside the court Dill is given a Coke by Mr Dolphus Raymond, a rich white man who prefers to live with blacks. When the children return to court Atticus is speaking to the jury, making it clear to them that Tom is innocent, and the Ewells guilty. Mayella, and not Tom, made sexual advances. Bob, and not Tom, beat Mayella. As he concludes his speech Cal arrives, sent by Alexandra to report that the children are missing.

NOTES AND GLOSSARY:

the only English riding boots I had ever seen: Mr Raymond's expensive imported boots are a sign of his aristocratic background

a run-of-the-mill man: an ordinary man

This case is as simple as black and white: Atticus's words are extremely ironic in context, as there is nothing simple about 'black' and 'white' in Maycomb county

Not an old Uncle: it was the custom in white Southern households to give elderly black male servants the title of Uncle

Thomas Jefferson: Jefferson (1743–1826), third President of the United States, author of the Declaration of Independence, which declares that 'all men are created equal'

the distaff side of the Executive branch: 'distaff' signifies 'female', and the reference here is to Mrs Eleanor Roosevelt, wife of President Roosevelt. She was a keen campaigner for Civil Rights

Rockefeller: J.D. Rockefeller (1839–1937), oil millionaire

Einstein: Albert Einstein (1879–1955), physicist, originator of the theory of relativity

Chapter twenty-one

When Atticus realises his children are in the courtroom he sends them home, but they beg permission to return after supper to hear the verdict. Jem is convinced that Atticus has won, but when the jury returns after several hours' deliberation they declare Tom guilty.

NOTES AND GLOSSARY:

I looked around. They were standing: the blacks rise to their feet in sign of respect as Atticus leaves the court

Chapter twenty-two

Jem cries and Atticus himself seems discouraged, but the next morning he assures the children that he will appeal against the verdict. The black community send gifts of food to Atticus to express their gratitude. Bob Ewell meets Atticus in the street and spits at him, threatening revenge.

NOTES AND GLOSSARY:

the White House: the official residence of the President of the United States

pickled pigs' knuckles: a favourite food among black Americans. Atticus is suggesting his sister will consider them too low-class for him to eat

Did Atticus put us up there as a sort of —?: Miss Stephanie Crawford's unfinished questions indicate the vulgarity of her mind. She guesses that Atticus deliberately put his children in the coloured balcony; she thinks it must have been uncomfortable sitting with the blacks because of their smell, and she wonder whether Scout understood the sexual references in the trial

Everyone one of 'em oughta be ridin' broomsticks: according to tradition, witches ride on broomsticks

Chapter twenty-three

The children are alarmed by Bob Ewell's threats, but Atticus reassures them. He explains that Tom was condemned entirely on account of racial prejudice, but agrees with Miss Maudie that the length of time taken by the jury to reach a verdict was a hopeful sign. He also reveals that the member of the jury who sided with himself was a Cunningham. Scout instantly resolves to invite Walter Cunningham to the house, but Aunt Alexandra forbids it, as the Cunninghams' social status is too low.

he was rarin' for: he was eager for

a hung jury: a jury unable to reach a verdict

yappy ... tacky: of inferior social status

fiddlin': local Southern country music, produced on an instrument halfway between a guitar and a violin

Cajuns: descendants of the original French settlers in the Louisiana territory

pot-liquor: the juice in which vegetables, especially turnip-greens, have been boiled. Aunt Alexandra believes that liking it is another indication of inferiority

hipped on: enthusiastic about

Chapter twenty-four

Aunt Alexandra entertains the Ladies' Missionary Circle to tea. While they are busy criticising Atticus's defence of Tom news arrives that Tom has been shot dead while attempting to escape from prison.

NOTES AND GLOSSARY:

Fighting the good fight: a quotation from a Christian hymn in which life is compared to a battle

when their time came: at childbirth

the preacher's wife's . . . : the ladies are spreading news of the preacher's wife's latest pregnancy

a card: a witty or amusing person

in stately largo: in a slow, impressive manner

there's no lady safe in her bed: this is another indication of white fear of black sexuality

His food doesn't stick going down: Miss Maudie draws attention to the impoliteness of criticising Atticus at the moment of enjoying the hospitality of his house

People up there: Northerners

that Mrs Roosevelt: in 1936 Mrs Roosevelt, wife of the President, defied the segregation law by deliberately placing her chair in the central aisle dividing black from white at a meeting in Birmingham, Alabama. As the Missionary Circle's meeting takes place in 1935, Harper Lee has made a slight slip here

the various whalebone ridges: Aunt Alexandra's corsets are made of whalebone

Are you together again?: have you regained self-control?

Chapter twenty-five

Dill recounts to Scout the scene that he and Jem witnessed when Atticus broke the news of Tom's death to his widow. Bob Ewell continues to threaten revenge.

NOTES AND GLOSSARY:

that English Channel of gossip: the English Channel, between England and France, is a busy trade route. Similarly, Miss Stephanie is a busy gossip route

Chapter twenty-six

School reopens, and the white community continues to discuss the Robinson case. In a Current Events class Scout is reminded of the problem of race relations by a discussion of Hitler's treatment of the Jews.

NOTES AND GLOSSARY:
Hidy do:	how do you do, how are you?
right pretty spell:	fine weather
Grit Paper:	grits (boiled corn grains) are a favourite Southern food, popular with poor white farmers. The *Grit Paper* is circulated by mail order in the South
holly roller:	member of an extreme evangelical Protestant sect
Elmer Davis:	a popular newscaster of the 1930s
Shoot:	go ahead

Chapter twenty-seven

Bob Ewell gets a government job, is dismissed for laziness, attempts to break into Judge Taylor's house, and molests Tom's widow. As Hallowe'en approaches the white community plans a pageant illustrating Maycomb history. Scout is to perform the role of ham, or 'Pork'.

NOTES AND GLOSSARY:
Tom Robinson was as forgotten as Boo Radley:	the parallel between two major characters is here made explicit
chunked at her:	threw things at her
Cotton Tom Heflin:	a notoriously conservative senator from Alabama
NRA:	the National Recovery Act of 1933. It was part of Roosevelt's New Deal Programme to combat the Depression, and included recognition of the right to collective bargaining. This was unpopular with powerful businessmen, and in 1935 the nine Supreme Court judges declared almost all of the Act unconstitutional
Hallowe'en:	31 October, the ancient Celtic festival of the Dead, when witches are supposed to be active, incorporated into Christian ritual as All Souls' Day. In the United States children traditionally play pranks on Hallowe'en
Misses Tutti and Frutti:	these nicknames come from a popular brand of Italian ice-cream, tutti-frutti, meaning all-fruit-flavoured

dog Victrolas: old fashioned record players whose trademark was a dog shown listening to a loudspeaker

there was not a barefooted child to be seen in Maycomb: the children wore shoes to put the hounds off their scent

apple-bobbing: a game in which players have to pick up apples floating in a tub of water, using only their teeth

taffy-pulling: Taffy is toffee, a sticky candy made with sugar and water. When pulled it stretches and hardens

pinning the tail on the donkey: a game in which blindfolded players are asked to pin the tail in the correct position on a picture of a donkey

Ad Astra per Aspera: a Latin phrase meaning 'To the stars through difficulties'. It was adopted as the Kansas State motto in 1861

somebody just walked over my grave: I felt a premonition of disaster

our longest journey together: it is their longest journey because it takes them to the brink of death

---

Chapter twenty-eight

During the performance of the pageant Scout falls asleep, misses her cue, and wakes up to make a late entrance in the middle of the grand finale. As she and Jem walk home in the dark they are followed and attacked just outside the Radley house. Scout is protected by the wire frame of her ham costume, but Jem's arm is broken. An unknown man intervenes to save them, and carries Jem to the Finch house. The doctor and sheriff are summoned, and the latter informs Atticus that Bob Ewell is lying dead with a knife in his heart.

NOTES AND GLOSSARY:

home-made divinity: a sort of fudge made with egg-whites

that means . . . from mud to the stars: Mrs Merriweather mistranslates her title, showing the weakness of her intellectual pretensions

to ascertain from its lichen which way was south: Colonel Maycomb is following the tradition that lichen grows on the north side of tree-trunks

Dixie: the favourite marching song of the Confederate Army. It later became an unofficial Southern national anthem

Chapter twenty-nine

Scout relates what happened to the sheriff. When he asks her to identify the unknown man who helped them she looks up and sees that it was Arthur Radley, who is now standing quietly in a corner of the room.

NOTES AND GLOSSARY:
meant business: (here) really intended murder
before you can pay hidy to 'em: before you can treat them as human beings
his torn denim shirt: though the Radleys are rich, Arthur is very poorly dressed

Chapter thirty

Atticus and the sheriff discuss the evening's events. At first Atticus thinks Jem knifed Bob Ewell, and is anxious that the affair should not be hushed up, as he does not want to claim special exemption from the law for his son. The sheriff then explains that Arthur Radley was the killer, and Atticus agrees that it will be better to avoid publicity by reporting that Ewell fell on his own knife and died by accident.

NOTES AND GLOSSARY:
the living-room lights were awfully strong: even in his anxiety Atticus remembers that Arthur is shy and prefers to avoid bright lights

Chapter thirty-one

After the discussions Scout escorts Arthur home. As she stands on the Radley porch she reflects on the experiences of the last two years before returning home to be put to bed by Atticus.

NOTES AND GLOSSARY:
she would see Arthur Radley escorting me: like her father, Scout is considerate. She wishes to preserve Arthur's dignity in the eyes of the neighbours, and so avoids leading him in public by the hand as if he were a child

Part 3

Commentary

General purpose

In *To Kill a Mockingbird*, Harper Lee presents a vivid picture of small-town Southern life in the 1930s. It is an affectionate and humorous picture, but is not without a darker side, since a major theme of the book is the evil of racialism.

The climax of the book comes in Part Two, in the trial of a black man falsely accused of rape. Everything which precedes or follows the trial, including the whole of Part One, is intended to build up a full understanding of the moral and social significance of that central event. The problem of racialism is thus a major concern in the book, and since racialism may be said to triumph at the end in the undeserved death of Tom Robinson, the book might seem tragic in its final effect. However, this is not the case. Though sometimes the good characters are reduced to despair, the book's ultimate conclusion is not despairing.

At some points in the novel evil seems stronger than good. When Dill cries at what he sees in the courtroom Mr Raymond tells him he is right to cry, since the world is so cruel. ' "Cry about the simple hell people give other people—without even thinking. Cry about the hell white people give coloured folks, without even stopping to think that they're people too" ' (Chapter 20). After the trial Jem too cries, and asks: ' "How could they do it, how could they?" ' Atticus for once has no consoling answer. He replies: ' "I don't know, but they did it. They've done it before and they did it tonight and they'll do it again and when they do it—seems only children weep" ' (Chapter 22). If this were Harper Lee's final judgement the novel would be predominantly gloomy in its effect, but in fact she has taken pains to emphasise a more optimistic side of the picture. Except at very rare moments of discouragement like that cited above Atticus has faith in the basic goodness of human nature. After Walter Cunningham has brought a lynch mob to attack him his comment is: ' "Mr Cunningham's basically a good man . . . he just has his blind spots like the rest of us" ' (Chapter 16). He is encouraged by the fact that the lynch mob went away, because, as he says: ' "That proves something—that a gang of wild animals *can* be stopped, simply because they're still human" '. Even when Bob Ewell has tried to kill the children Atticus wants to find some excuse for him. He tells the sheriff that Ewell must have been ' "out of his mind" ' (Chapter 29).

The book as a whole tends to support Atticus's general view of human nature. The basic goodness is seen most clearly in the innocence of children: Jem and Dill weep for injustice; Scout is instinctively egalitarian; the entire first-grade class instantly rushes to comfort an unpopular teacher when she cries. Even Tom's case gives ground for hope. Judge Taylor, Heck Tate and Link Deas are on Tom's side; even Mr Underwood, who despises Negroes, is ready to stand up for justice. Before the trial he is prepared to defend Atticus from the lynch mob; after Tom's death he publishes an editorial condemning his 'senseless slaughter' (Chapter 25). The fact that the jury took so long to reach their decision is encouraging; as Miss Maudie tells the children: '"... I thought to myself, well, we're making a step—it's just a baby step, but it's a step"' (Chapter 22). Atticus agrees with her. '"That was the one thing that made me think, well, this may be the shadow of a beginning. That jury took a few hours"' (Chapter 23). Maycomb County is full of prejudice, but there are signs of change and progress, so Harper Lee is justified in ending the book on an optimistic note. On the last page Atticus reads Scout to sleep with a story about a boy wrongfully suspected of various crimes. Scout murmurs sleepily: '"An' they chased him 'n' never could catch him, 'cause they didn't know what he looked like, an' Atticus, when they finally saw him, why he hadn't done any of those things ... Atticus, he was real nice"'. Her father replies, summing up the book's final message '"Most people are, Scout, when you finally see them"' (Chapter 31).

The comic element

The cheerful but serious note with which the novel closes suits the novel's basic purpose: entertainment mixed with moral gravity. The humour is an essential part of the effect the book creates; it is sustained all through the action, even at the most painful crises. In the trial scene, for instance, Scout gives a comic description of the judge's cigar-chewing. The reader is bound to smile as he reads *To Kill a Mockingbird*, and the variety of comedy is wide.

Harper Lee makes fun of all aspects of Maycomb County, starting with its history, which includes drunken surveyors who sited the town in the wrong place and a stupid founding father, Colonel Maycomb, who could not tell south from north but who is revered as a great man by county inhabitants. The complacency of the provincial society is mocked, especially the stupid self-satisfaction of the ladies, most clearly displayed in the account of the missionary tea in Chapter 24.

As well as mocking the society in general the author provides a large number of amusingly eccentric characters such as the fat, pompous Mr Avery and the foolish, hysterical Misses Tutti and Frutti. Even though some of these individuals may appear on only one occasion the descriptions of them are so lively that they make a very vivid impression.

Comic incidents abound, as well as comic characters. A typical example is Scout's performance in the role of 'Pork' at the Maycomb County Pageant.

A further variety of humour is verbal. Examples may be found in the dry wit of Atticus, the waspish tongue of Miss Maudie, and Harper Lee's own ironic manner of narration. Atticus, for instance, tells the filthy Dill that in the interests of preventing soil erosion he should '"put some of the county back where it belongs"' (Chapter 14).

Finally, a note of humour is provided all through the novel by the use of Scout as narrator. What amuses us are her naïvety, directness and frank speech. Even at tense moments in the action her approach can raise a smile,as it does when she tries to make polite conversation about entailments to a lynch mob. In general the auther has succeeded in preserving a light tone and entertaining atmosphere all through the book, even though the underlying theme is both sad and serious.

The underlying morality

Comedy forms only one part of the effect of *To Kill a Mockingbird*. Its author is also concerned to present certain universal moral truths. Most prominent among these are the need to respect the sanctity of life, the need for love, and the need for tolerance and understanding.

Respect for the sanctity of life is a feature of all the characters Harper Lee admires. The majority of the white community cares nothing for the life of a black man, but Atticus values the life even of a bird. He refuses to touch a gun except in cases of absolute necessity, because he feels his skill gives him an unfair advantage over most living things. His son seems to take after him. When Jem builds a snowman he carefully preserves the lives of all the earthworms he digs up, and when Scout is tormenting a roly-poly insect he orders her to stop. Dill, too, feels sympathy for all living creatures. He tells Jem that striking a match under a turtle is hateful. Miss Maudie's sympathy extends even to plants; she 'loved everything that grew in God's earth, even the weeds' (Chapter 5). This need for respect for all forms of life is emphasised in the title *To Kill a Mockingbird*, whose symbolic significance will be discussed later.

The need of all humans for love is most clearly shown in the pathetic stories of Arthur Radley and Dill, both of whom are deprived of family warmth. The cruelty of old Mr Radley inspires Cal, who never criticises white people, to spit when his coffin passes. Dill's parents are not positively cruel, but their generosity with material gifts cannot conceal their real indifference. As he says, '"they just wasn't interested in me"' (Chapter 14). It is because he is starved of love at home that Dill tries to make a new family for himself. He proposes marriage to Scout and suggests they get a baby. Though his circumstances are superficially very different from Arthur's he instinctively sympathises with him, because he can understand the loneliness of a person whose family does not care for him. The unhappiness of Dill and Arthur is contrasted with the warmth and security of the Finch family life. Scout and Jem are safe, because they know their father loves them. When Scout sees Mayella in court, and realises that her family give her no support or affection, she thinks Mayella must be 'the loneliest person in the world' (Chapter 19). Everyone needs love. It is because Mayella receives no love from her family that she turns to a black man who has been kind to her, and so precipitates the tragedy of his trial and death.

The main moral lesson Scout and the readers learn in the course of the novel is the need to be tolerant towards others. At the beginning Atticus tells her: '"You can never really understand a person until you consider things from his point of view ... until you climb into his skin and walk around in it"' (Chapter 3). At the end she knows this by experience. Standing on the Radley porch she realises what she has learned: 'Atticus was right. One time he said you never really know a man until you stand in his shoes and walk around in them. Just standing on the Radley porch was enough' (Chapter 31). The process has been gradual. At the beginning she and Jem saw Arthur as a freak, and not a human being at all. The events of the novel have made her understand her father's words. On the night of the lynch mob, for instance, Atticus and Tom are saved because, as Atticus says: '"... you children last night made Walter Cunningham stand in my shoes for a minute"' (Chapter 16). It is only by the imaginative effort to stand in others' shoes that human beings can become tolerant.

These lessons on the sanctity of life, the need for love and for tolerant understanding may be combined into a single message: that all human beings belong together and need each other. To have divisions between men is stupid, since all men are one family. Harper Lee underlines this point by creating a network of unexpected connections between characters who on the surface are not at all similar, but who on a deeper level prove to have much in common. The parallel between Arthur and Dill has already been mentioned. Jem and Tom also form a symbolic pair, linked by their injured left arms. The white Miss Maudie is joined to the black community in their reactions after the trial when all of them rise early to prepare food for the Finch family. These links and parallels help to drive home the idea that since we are all human beings we are joined together. Everybody belongs; even the mad freak Arthur turns out to be the best friend and neighbour anyone could wish to have.

To Kill a Mockingbird is both comic and serious. We laugh as we read it, but the humour is a subtle technique for conveying the serious message painlessly. Harper Lee has very skillfully blended light entertainment with serious morality.

The historical and social context

While some knowledge of the Civil War and its aftermath is essential to proper understanding of this novel, other background information is useful, especially that relating to the economic conditions in the 1930s and the distinctive qualities of Southern culture, including attitudes to race, religion, social class and sexual stereotypes.

The economic background

Maycomb County, as the author describes it, is in a state of economic decline. The town is shabby; as the author says in the first chapter: 'Maycomb was an old town, but it was a tired old town when I first knew it. In rainy weather the streets turned to red slop; grass grew on the sidewalks, the courthouse sagged in the square' (Chapter 1). Communications with outlying houses depend on dirt roads; and all the county inhabitants, whether professional people or farmers, are poor.

There are two reasons for this economic decline: the general decay of Southern prosperity after the Civil War, and the immediate effects of the Wall Street crash of 1929. The whole country was involved in the Depression following the crash, but the South, and the rural sector in particular, suffered most severely: Atticus explains to Jem, when he asks if the Finches are as poor as the Cunninghams, '"The Cunninghams are country folks, farmers, and the crash hit them hardest"'. He goes on to explain that '"professional people were poor because the farmers were poor. As Maycomb County was farm country, nickels and dimes were hard to come by for doctors and dentists and lawyers"' (Chapter 2). The novel is set at the time of Roosevelt's New Deal programme, which was intended to combat the worst effects of the Depression by providing jobs for the unemployed. But the New Deal seems to have little effect in Maycomb County. As Scout reports in Chapter 12, time passes but 'bread lines in the cities grew longer, people in the country grew poorer.'

The harsh economic conditions in Maycomb may help to explain, if not excuse, the cruel behaviour of its inhabitants. Men like Walter Cunningham are embittered by poverty. In their state of insecurity their fear and hatred of blacks are increased, and violence comes naturally. Moreover, the fact that Maycomb, as a declining Southern town, has been cut off from the main stream of American life accounts for the backwardness and narrow-mindedness of its citizens. As Atticus says, they are simply ignorant.

Traditional Southern culture: race, religion, class and sex

Southerners pride themselves on their possession of a unique cultural tradition. Harper Lee's own attitude to this tradition is critical but affectionate; she shows its shortcomings but does so, usually, in a comic light. In the case of the cultural tradition of racialism, however, she adopts a more serious tone.

Racialism

Racialism, according to Atticus, is '"Maycomb County's usual disease"', and Maycomb people '"go stark raving mad when anything involving a Negro comes up"' (Chapter 9). Their instinctive conviction is that '"*all* Negroes lie, that *all* Negroes are basically immoral beings, that *all* Negro men are not to be trusted around our women"' (Chapter 20). Since Atticus knows Maycomb people think like this, he knows in advance that the jury will never accept Tom Robinson's word against that of a white man. Tom is found guilty in the face of all the evidence which proves his innocence. His conviction, however, is only the extreme example of racial injustice in Maycomb. The blacks are deprived of educational opportunities; only four members of the congregation at Cal's church are literate. Their job prospects are limited. Zeebo has an exceptionally good job for a black, and he is only a garbage collector. Their wages are wretched; Mrs Merriweather pays her maid only $1.25 for a full week's work. Black life is cheap in white eyes. When it is reported that Mr Nathan Radley has shot at a Negro in his garden no one criticises his action. When Tom dies the majority of the white community feels no pity. For them his death is only another example of the stupidity of black people.

In spite of this general scene of racial injustice, Harper Lee offers some hope that attitudes may be changing. Characters like Miss Maudie always speak of black people with respect, using terms like 'Negroes' or 'coloured folks' rather than the derogatory 'niggers'. She tells Jem at the time of the trial that there is at least '"a handful of people in this town who say fair play is not marked White only"' (Chapter 24). Atticus believes that in a higher court, even a higher Southern court, Tom stands a good chance of being acquitted. These are tiny signs, but hopeful in the Southern context.

Religion

The Christian religion is an essential element in Southern culture. Going to church, according to Scout, is 'Maycomb's principal recreation' (Chapter 1); the social life of the ladies is centred on the Missionary Circle; the Baptist/Methodist football match is such a popular event that 'everybody in town's father was playing, it seemed, except Atticus'

(Chapter 10). Harper Lee, however, does not feel that organised religion is a force for good in Maycomb society, at least among the whites.

The white community boasts of being Christian, but its behaviour does not conform to Christian ideals. Simon Finch, the founder of the Finch family, professed to be a pious Methodist but owned slaves and was notoriously mean. Miss Maudie's strict Baptists consider themselves supremely religious but are so lacking in Christian charity that they assure her that she will burn in hell because she spends too much time working in her garden. The ladies of the Missionary Circle congratulate themselves on losing no opportunity to 'witness for the Lord''' (Chapter 24), but their attitude to black people in general, and to the Robinson family in particular, is grotesquely unchristian. When Scout hears them discussing the need for some unnamed woman to reform her way of life she naturally believes they are talking of Mayella Ewell. In fact, however, the unnamed woman to whom they wish to extend their gracious forgiveness is the innocent Helen Robinson.

For Harper Lee most members of the White Protestant sects in Maycomb are not true Christians at all. As Jem says, the members of the jury who convict Tom are 'heathen' (Chapter 22). However, her intention is to satirise not the Christian faith itself, but only those people who profess it but fail to practise it. There do exist some real Christians in Maycomb. Atticus, for instance, tells Scout that his religion obliges him to defend Tom Robinson, even though he knows his action will be unpopular. '"Scout, I couldn't go to church and worship God if I didn't try to help that man"' (Chapter 11). Apart from Atticus the only people in the book who really put their religion into practice are the black community. When Jem and Scout visit Cal's church in Chapter 12 they see the Christian ideal of love and responsibility for one's neighbour in action. Reverend Sykes appeals for help for the Robinson family and then closes the church doors so that no one can leave until sufficient money has been collected. The black community is living its religion; the white community simply talks about it.

Social class

Maycomb society is strictly stratified. Aunt Alexandra is angry when she learns that the children have attended Cal's church, and is unwilling to invite little Walter Cunningham to the house. In her eyes poor whites and blacks are unfit to associate with the Finch family. Jem once tries to explain Maycomb social structure to his sister. '"The thing about it is, our kind of folks don't like the Cunninghams, the Cunninghams don't like the Ewells, and the Ewells hate and despise the coloured folks"' (Chapter 23). Scout, in her childish innocence, rejects this analysis. '"Naw, Jem, I think there's just one kind of folks. Folks."' In an ideal world she would be right, but Jem is old enough to realise that the world is not so simple. '"If there's just one kind of folks, why can't they get on with each other? If they're all alike, why do they go out of their way to despise each other?"' (Chapter 23).

The two children attempt throughout the book to find a rational basis for class distinctions. Scout begins with a simple practical definition. She believes 'fine folks were people who did the best they could with the sense they had'. Aunt Alexandra, however, takes the traditional Southern view that high social status depends on hereditary land-ownership. As Scout puts it, 'the longer a family had been squatting on one patch of land the finer it was' (Chapter 13). Atticus disagrees; he believes that 'most of this old family stuff's foolishness because everybody's family's just as old as everybody else's' (Chapter 23). Jem then formulates the theory that social standing depends on education. '"Background doesn't mean Old Family ... I think it's how long your family's been readin' and writin'"' (Chapter 23). Scout is still not convinced, and it is Miss Maudie who has the last word. For her, status is a matter of morality, and the people whom she considers have 'background' in Maycomb are '"the handful of people who say a fair trial is for everybody, not just us"' (Chapter 24). Harper Lee agrees with her. She believes a person's true social status should be determined by his moral character. There are two men in the novel whom she regards as real gentlemen. One is Atticus, who is 'civilized in his heart' (Chapter 10); the other is Tom Robinson, whose testimony in court makes Scout realise that 'in their own way, Tom Robinson's manners were as good as Atticus's' (Chapter 19).

Sexual stereotypes: Southern manhood and Southern womanhood
Another focus for Southern pride was what Southerners considered to be the special manliness of their men and the special womanliness of their women. Their conception of proper masculine and feminine roles was highly exaggerated, but it became elevated in their minds to an almost mythical status, and they came to feel that Southerners should conform to Southern sexual stereotypes.

Men in the South valued reckless courage highly and had an exaggerated concern for honour. Southern manliness involved hot temper, quickness to take offence, and contempt for human life, whether one's own or that of others. Proper manly behaviour was bold, wild and swaggering. Women, on the other hand, were meant to act and look like the most delicate flowers: pure, fragile, helpless and in need of constant masculine protection. In the early chapters of *To Kill a Mockingbird* Harper Lee shows how deeply these notions permeate Southern society. All the little boys in Scout's class instinctively rush to the aid of their teacher when they think she is frightened by a mouse. She is a Southern female and they are Southern males; so their duty is to protect her even though she is twice their size and probably three times their age. It is to the same conditioned instinct that Mayella appeals in the courtroom when she says: '"That nigger yonder took advantage of me, an' if you fine fancy gentlemen don't wanta do nothin' about it then you're all yellow stinkin' cowards, the lot of you"' (Chapter 18).

Harper Lee has little time for the Southern sexual stereotypes. When the book opens both Scout and Jem are infected by the idea of 'manly' behaviour. Anything is preferable to the imputation of cowardice. Jem, though terrified to approach the Radley house, has to do so when dared by Dill because 'he loved honour more than his head' (Chapter 1). Scout, not yet grown up into the feminine world, accepts the masculine ideal of physical courage for herself and suffers deeply when Atticus forbids her to fight. Both children feel embarrassed by their father's lack of 'manliness'. As Scout explains: 'He did not do the things our school-mates' fathers did: he never went hunting, he did not play poker or fish or drink or smoke' (Chapter 10). Jem is shamed by his father's failure to play football for the Methodists, as it seems to show him up as a weakling. But as the plot develops the children's idea of what constitutes true manhood is modified. First, the rabid dog incident shows them their father is the best shot in the country, though his gentleness and modesty, in contrast to the swaggering Southern ideal, have kept it secret from them. Gradually Scout comes to appreciate that physical courage is not the only sort of courage. When she sees Atticus with Mrs Dubose she reflects that 'my father, who hated guns and had never been to any wars, was the bravest man who ever lived' (Chapter 11). Then Atticus explains why he wanted them to spend time with Mrs Dubose: '"I wanted you to see something about her—I wanted you to see what real courage is, instead of getting the idea that courage is a man with a gun in his hand"' (Chapter 11). Atticus himself, Scout realises, is a truly courageous man, even though he does not outwardly conform to the idea of Southern manhood.

The problem of proper womanly behaviour is more complex. Harper Lee clearly sympathises with the feminist movement, and yet in the end she makes Scout conform, at least to some degree, to conventional ladylike behaviour. At the start Scout does not want to be a girl. She prefers trousers to dresses; she resents being left out of the urination competition between Dill and Jem, and she can always be enraged by her brother's telling her she is acting like a girl. Aunt Alexandra is an enemy, because she wants to transform Scout into a conventional little girl. Scout resists, but gradually comes to realise that sooner or later she will have to conform. At the Missionary Circle tea she reflects: 'There was no doubt about it, I must soon enter this world, where on its surface fragrant ladies rocked slowly, fanned gently, and drank cool water. . . . But I was more at home in my father's world' (Chapter 24). Later in the same scene she even comes to see that ladylike behaviour can be gallant and courageous. Aunt Alexandra and Miss Maudie, shattered by the news of Tom Robinson's death, pull themselves together and go back to behave politely to the ladies who have just insulted them by slighting references to Atticus's defence of Tom Robinson. Seeing their courage and dignity, Scout is moved to emulate them. 'I carefully picked up the tray and watched myself walk to Mrs Merriweather. With my very best company manners I asked her if she would have some. After all, if Aunty could be a lady at a time like this, so could I' (Chapter 24). But Aunt Alexandra does not have the last word. On the evening when Bob Ewell attacks the children she is so distraught that she actually tells Scout to put on her boyish overalls. '"Put these on, darling," she said, handing me the garments she most despised' (Chapter 28).

To some degree, then, Scout comes to conform to conventional femininity, but this does not mean that Harper Lee really accepts the traditional conception of the female role. One of her objections to organised Christianity is that it degrades and devalues women. Miss Maudie's Baptists 'think women a sin by definition' (Chapter 5), and even in Cal's church Scout hears the minister preach 'the Impurity of Women doctrine that seemed to preoccupy all clergymen' (Chapter 12). One of the defects in the Alabama legal system is that 'Miss Maudie can't serve on a jury because she's a woman' (Chapter 23). Like the blacks, women are an oppressed class in Southern society, though the complacent Missionary Circle ladies do not realise it.

The last word on this topic should go to Atticus, since on all issues he speaks for reason and decency. He punctiliously observes the conventions of courtesy accorded to women in the Southern tradition. When he approaches Tom Robinson's tiny daughter he gravely raises his hat to her. But, as he tells Aunt Alexandra, the ideals of Southern womanhood can be carried too far. He is '"in favour of Southern womanhood as much as anybody, but not for preserving polite fiction at the expense of human life"' (Chapter 15). The fiction here is that a white Southern woman could never possibly make sexual advances to any man, let alone to a black man. But Mayella Ewell has done so, and the polite pretence that she has not is going to cost Tom his life. The extreme ideal of Southern womanhood, like that of Southern manhood, has no place in the real world.

Structure

To Kill a Mockingbird is divided into two parts: Part One, which runs from Chapter 1 to Chapter 12, and Part Two, which runs from Chapter 13 to Chapter 31. Part Two is longer than Part One, and also more clearly focused on the novel's major concern, the tragedy of race relations in the South. This concern is mentioned in Part One, but for the most part other affairs hold the centre of the stage. Part Two, however, is almost entirely taken up with Tom's case. From Chapter 15 onwards attention is steadily focused either on the trial itself or on matters arising from the trial. Even Chapter 26, which on the surface describes the routine life of the children in the autumn after the trial, is actually related to the Robinson case because it raises the question of racial prejudice by way of a Current Events class at Scout's school. Comparison of Parts One and Two might therefore make it seem as if the novel lacked unity, since Part One is partly concerned with matters other than the race relations which are the subject of Part Two. However, this is not so. Harper Lee gives a hint of her plan on the first page, when she reports Jem's theory that the story begins in the summer when Dill first came to Maycomb, two years before the trial. Jem is quite right.

The reason the novel begins in summer 1933 rather than, say, November 1934 when the alleged rape takes place, is that Harper Lee wants to do more than merely relate the facts of Tom's trial, conviction and death. She wants us to understand the whole social background of the case, so that we shall know not only what happened, but also why it happened, how it happened and whether it could or should ever happen again. To accomplish this she uses the point of view of a child. Scout is too young to understand the situation straight away. She needs time to learn about the adult world. In a sense the novel is about growing up, the moral education which Scout and Jem must undergo if Tom's trial is not to scar them emotionally for life. As Atticus tells his brother before the trial: '"You know what's going to happen as well as I do, Jack, and I hope and pray I can get Jem and Scout through it without bitterness, and, most of all, without catching Maycomb's usual disease"' (Chapter 9). What happens in Part One is the children's insurance against such bitterness and disease; they are being prepared, unconsciously, for what is to come. Moreover, the reader is sharing in the preparation. Since we see through the eyes of an innocent child we have to recognise the irrationality of adult attitudes to class and race. This process of moral education is part of what makes the episodes in Part One relevant to the events of Part Two.

If any one figure dominates Part One it is Arthur Radley. As Tom's situation is the main centre of interest in Part Two, Arthur's situation is the main centre of interest in Part One. More than half of Part One is taken up with the children's efforts to contact him, just as more than half of Part Two is concerned with Tom's trial. This shift in interest might seem like poor planning, but close examination will reveal that Arthur and Tom have much in common. Neither is accepted as a human being by the community at large. Arthur is considered a crazy freak; Tom, just because he is black, is little better than an animal in the eyes of the whites.

Harper Lee shows in both cases how wrong the community is. Tom, as his testimony in court demonstrates, is not only a human being but a far better human being than the jury who convict him. Arthur, far from being a monster, acts like a father to Jem and Scout. This is particularly poignant, since Arthur's own father rejected him. Similarly Tom, who receives only cruelty from the white community, is the only man to offer kindness to the poor white Mayella. Both he and Arthur are victims of pride and prejudice. They belong together in one book; their histories illustrate the same tragic point.

Apart from the Radley episodes the main incidents in Part One are Miss Maudie's fire, the rabid dog adventure and the encounter with Mrs Dubose. All three provide valuable moral lessons for the children. From Miss Maudie and Mrs Dubose they learn the meaning of courage. Miss Maudie accepts the loss of all she has without complaint; Mrs Dubose endures agony to break her drug-addiction. When Atticus shoots the rabid dog the children see the nature of truly civilised behaviour, modest rather than boastful, gentle rather than aggressive. Jem's visits to Mrs Dubose give him a chance to practise such civilised conduct for himself. He learns to control his temper and act like a gentleman in spite of her provocation. By experiences like these the children learn how to endure suffering, how to retain dignity, and how to respect the rights of others. At the time of the trial these lessons help them to survive. Scout even says, when the trial is over and the children are exposed to the community's gossip and criticism of Atticus: 'In a way, it was like the era of Mrs Henry Lafayette Dubose, without all her yelling' (Chapter 26). None of the early episodes, then, is irrelevant to the moral scheme of the book as a whole.

Careful analysis reveals that *To Kill a Mockingbird* is firmly constructed, each episode contributing to the whole. Harper Lee helps us to understand the total pattern by the summary she gives in the final chapter, when Scout stands on the Radley porch and thinks over the events of the past two years.

Characterisation

One of the chief attractions of this novel is its wide range of lively characters. To analyse each one separately would take a very long time, but fortunately the nature of Maycomb society makes this unnecessary. Maycomb County is a small community, and has been isolated in the years following the Civil War. Social patterns have remained static, and the society is divided into clearly defined groups. Family loyalties are specially intense; when Aunt Alexandra is trying to instill family pride into the children she 'never let a chance escape her to point out the shortcomings of other tribal groups to the greater glory of our own'

(Chapter 13). Maycomb family resemblances are strong. Scout reports that 'the older citizens, the present generation of people who had lived side by side for years and years, were utterly predictable to each other: they took for granted attitudes, character shading, even gestures, as having been repeated in each generation and refined by time' (Chapter 13).

Other tightly knit groups in Maycomb are bound not by ties of blood but by social class or religious affiliation. Harper Lee defines the strict social stratification in Maycomb as sort of a caste system, and the separate castes do not mix socially. In addition, religious differences matter; the Baptists play football against the Methodists; the strict sects such as Mennonites and footwashers keep themselves apart from all the other Protestants. As well as this each individual tends to belong to some special clique or club within his own social group. The rich white ladies have their Missionary Circle; the old men who sit round the courthouse square have their Idlers Club; the black people have their own church, Missionary Society and sewing circle.

All these social divisions make it possible to analyse Maycomb characters on a group basis, by family, class, race and club. There are only two significant outsiders in the novel: Dill, who is not a full-time Maycomb resident but who becomes almost a member of the family during his summer vacations, and Mr Raymond, who belongs by birth to the rich white group but who prefers to live with the black. He is the only character in the novel who has crossed the strict class and race frontiers in Maycomb society.

Atticus Finch

The character of Atticus Finch is well summed up by Miss Maudie when she calls him 'civilised in his heart' (Chapter 10). He stands for all that is best in Maycomb as a citizen, a father, a Christian and a Southern gentleman.

As a citizen Atticus is highly responsible and highly respected. He is elected unopposed to the state legislature, and works hard for it. Miss Maudie speaks for the community when she tells Aunt Alexandra, '"Whether Maycomb knows it or not, we're paying him the highest tribute we can pay a man. We trust him to do right"' (Chapter 24). His conduct and conversation throughout the book show that he is entirely free from the usual Maycomb faults of pride, racialism and hypocrisy.

As a father Atticus stands in contrast to Mr Radley and Bob Ewell, both of whom ill-treat their offspring. Scout and Jem have perfect confidence in their father. He always tells them the truth, and they are totally secure in the knowledge that he loves them. When they fear he is in danger from Bob Ewell they cannot eat or play; when they fight it is to avenge not insults to themselves but rather insults to him. His steady reassuring presence in their lives is epitomised in the novel's last words, when he goes to sit and watch by Jem's bed. 'He turned out the light and went into Jem's room. He would be there all night, and he would be there when Jem waked up in the morning' (Chapter 31).

Atticus is also a truly religious man, who puts into practice Christian teaching on love, tolerance and forgiveness of others. As he tells Scout, '"I do my best to love everybody"' (Chapter 11). He teaches his children not to bear grudges and tries to find excuses even for his enemies. Instead of hating and despising Mayella he feels sorry for her. As Miss Maudie says, he represents true Christian values in Maycomb. '"We're so rarely called on to be Christians, but when we are, we've got men like Atticus to go for us"' (Chapter 22).

Finally, Atticus represents the admirable side of the tradition of the Southern gentleman. He is supremely courteous to all females, even the evil-tongued old Mrs Dubose. When Walter Cunningham comes to lunch he speaks to him as politely as he would to a man of his own age and social status. He is brave, too, as a Southern gentleman should be. He faces the mad dog and risks his life to protect Tom from the lynch mob, but does so quietly, without any exhibitionist display.

Atticus's manner is cool and dry; his speech is formal, but his heart is warm. When he sees the food sent to his house by the black community he is so moved that his eyes fill with tears. He is invariably kind and considerate to others. At Miss Maudie's fire he is the one who remembers to rescue her favourite rocking-chair. He is Harper Lee's ideal of a true gentleman and a true hero.

Jem

Jem is very much his father's son, and through the novel his resemblance to Atticus increases. From the beginning he is like his father in his consideration for others; when he first meets Dill he quickly realises that Dill is embarrassed by his parents' divorce, so he stops Scout asking awkward questions about it. It is he who thinks of inviting hungry Walter Cunningham to lunch; it is he who offers to help clear Miss Maudie's garden after the fire; it is he who notices when Atticus is worried and warns Scout, '"he's got a lot on his mind now, without us worrying him"' (Chapter 14).

Just as Atticus is a good father, Jem is a good elder brother. He takes care of Scout, comforts her when she is distressed, explains things to her when she is puzzled. When she eats the Radley chewing-gum he makes her gargle to prevent infection; when he is given money for his birthday he shares it with her; when she is miserable at having disgraced herself at the pageant he is so kind that she reflects that he 'was becoming almost as good as Atticus at making you feel right when things go wrong' (Chapter 28). Like Atticus he is compassionate to others—he weeps with pity for Arthur when Mr Nathan Radley puts cement in the hole in the tree, and when Scout asks him to explain racial discrimination he is so upset he cannot bear to discuss it.

Like his father Jem is clever. When there is not enough snow to build a complete snowman he has the idea of building it in earth and then covering it with a thin layer of snow, and when Atticus sees the result he says: '"... from now on I'll never worry about what'll become of you, son, you'll always have an idea"' (Chapter 8). At the trial he is one of the first to realise the point of Atticus's questions as to which side of Mayella's face was injured. After the trial he pleases his father by his intelligent questions about the jury system.

Jem suffers during the book, especially at the time of the trial when his reason and decency assure him that Atticus must win. It is clear, however, from his later discussions with his father that he is not overcome by the shock of defeat; already he is trying to work out ways of changing the Alabama law in order to prevent future miscarriages of justice. He is willing to persevere in spite of setbacks, just like his father.

Finally, it should be noticed that Jem's character develops as he grows older. At the beginning of the novel he shows signs of childlike immaturity—he fails to realise, for instance, that acting the Radley drama might cause distress to Arthur. Also, in the early chapters his idea of courage and manhood is very superficial, and he is ashamed of what he considers Atticus's physical feebleness. This changes, however, after the incident with the mad dog. Later he is able to appreciate the really heroic nature of the work Atticus does; he even understands that a cartoon making fun of Atticus in the *Montgomery Advertiser* is actually a compliment, since it shows his father 'spends his time doin' things that wouldn't get done if nobody did 'em' (Chapter 12). By the end of the book he has gained so much in maturity of understanding and behaviour that Miss Maudie, baking after the trial for all the three children, gives him a whole slice of the grown-up cake whereas Scout and Dill get only little separate cakes. All three children understand the significance of this.

Scout

Just as Jem is clearly Atticus Finch's son Scout is clearly Atticus Finch's daughter, but she is not so calmly rational as either her father or her brother. This is due partly to her age, but also to the fact that she is more naturally impulsive in her reactions. She rushes into fights, jumps to conclusions, and is in general more emotional than the males in her family. As Atticus puts it, '"... Scout'd just as soon jump on someone as look at him if her pride's at stake"' (Chapter 9).

Scout shares many of Atticus's moral principles, such as egalitarianism and anti-racialism, but she does so on a simple emotional basis. She wants to invite Walter Cunningham and to visit Cal just because she likes them and is instinctively without prejudice. Like her father and brother she is clever and loves reading. Atticus once tells her that she has a good head, though she does not always use it properly, simply because her emotions tend to run away with her. She also possesses the Finch courage. When Jem is forced to go to the Dubose house she insists on supporting him with her company even though she is terrified of Mrs Dubose. Like her male relatives, too, she is instinctively considerate of others; in fact she is the first of the children to feel uncomfortable about their Radley activities. At the very end there is a striking example of her sensitivity to others' feelings in her handling of Arthur Radley. She realises without any words from him that he would like to see Jem and to stroke his hair; and when the time comes for Arthur to return to the Radley house she is careful to preserve his public dignity by refusing to lead him like a child.

Even though she lacks her male relatives' calm and rational self-control Scout has some qualities in which she is their superior. She is extremely warm, friendly and open. Her natural instinct is to make friends with everyone she meets; in the centre of a dangerous lynch mob she makes pleasant conversation with Mr Cunningham in order to make him feel at home.

Like Jem, Scout gains in maturity as time passes. She learns some degree of self-control and refrains from fighting children who insult her father even though it shames her to do so: 'Somehow, if I fought Cecil I would let Atticus down' (Chapter 9). She develops deeper understanding of the needs and rights of other people; by the end of the book she feels real remorse at having taken part in what must have been sheer torment to Arthur Radley. Finally, though she is a natural tomboy, always wearing trousers for choice and disliking the company of ladies, she does gradually begin to adjust to the feminine role. Love and admiration for Cal initiate the process; when she watches Cal at work in the kitchen she says, 'I began to feel there was some skill involved in being a girl' (Chapter 12).

As in Jem's case, the process of development is often painful for Scout. She suffers, however, in ways rather different from his. He is most distressed by the betrayal of abstract principles of justice; she is hurt more by the conventional limitations of her sex and by the fact that her adored brother naturally grows away from her as he passes from childhood to adolescence. However, her experiences through the book have taught her many lessons. What she says at the end is a typical example of her childish over-simplification but it has some truth in it: 'As I made my way home, I thought Jem and I would get grown but there wasn't much else for us to learn, except possibly algebra' (Chapter 31).

Aunt Alexandra

Aunt Alexandra is Atticus's sister, but so unlike him in character that she makes Scout inclined to believe in folk-tales concerning changelings. Our earliest impressions of her are all unfavourable: she is so cold and unloving that she reminds Scout of Mount Everest; she shows the prejudices of Maycomb society so thoroughly that she 'fitted into the world of Maycomb like a hand into a glove' (Chapter 13). She annoys Scout by her snobbery and her insistence on ladylike behaviour; she even annoys the patient Atticus by her barely concealed racial prejudice, as when she tries to persuade him that Cal should be dismissed as a bad influence on the children. In fact her social instincts incline her to side with the Maycomb majority against Atticus; as Jem reports to Scout: '"She won't let him alone about Tom Robinson. She almost said Atticus was disgracin' the family"' (Chapter 15). In the first part of the book all that Scout can find in her favour is that she is an extremely good cook.

Towards the end of the novel, however, we begin to see a better side of Aunt Alexandra. She loves her brother and remains loyal to him in spite of her prejudice against his opinions. When he returns home from his defeat in the trial she greets him with the words: '"I'm sorry, brother"' (Chapter 22). Scout is impressed because she has never heard her aunt call Atticus 'brother' before. When he brings the news of Tom's death Aunt Alexandra almost breaks down, and she tells Miss Maudie: '"I can't say I approve of everything he does, Maudie, but he's my brother and I just want to know when this will ever end. ... It tears him to pieces"' (Chapter 24). It is on that same occasion that Scout sees her aunt's courage and dignity, when she goes back to face the ladies coolly and politely, as if nothing had happened. It is not until the very last pages that we realise that, after all, under her cold, forbidding exterior Aunt Alexandra has a good heart. When the children escape Bob Ewell's attack she starts demonstrating warm concern in a way she never has before. She even calls Scout 'darling'.

Dill

Dill, since he is not a full-time resident of Maycomb nor a member of the Finch family, is not so obviously and directly involved as his friends in the central tragedy of the Robinson case. In a way, however, he suffers more than either Jem or Scout. Unlike them, he lacks the security of family love; as Scout's cousin Francis unkindly says: '"... he hasn't got a home ... he just gets passed round from relative to relative ..."' (Chapter 9). His loneliness makes it natural that he, of all the children, is the most fascinated with the Radley house, which 'drew him as the moon draws water' (Chapter 1). This is because he is unconsciously aware of a similarity between his own situation and that of Arthur Radley. His 'engagement' to Scout, to whom he proposes marriage during his second summer in Maycomb, and his suggestion that they should get themselves a baby, are clearly symptoms of his desperate need to create for himself the family life which he lacks. Even his aunt Rachel, with whom he spends the summer, is not a person deserving a child's love, respect and trust. He is well aware of her secret drinking habits and her lack of real interest in himself.

Dill may not be as intellectually advanced as Jem, but he is more inventive. Like Scout he can express himself in vivid images, as when he describes Helen Robinson's reaction to the news of her husband's death: '"Scout ... she just fell down in the dirt ... like a giant with a big foot just came along and stepped on her. Just ump—" Dill's fat foot hit the ground. "Like you'd step on an ant"' (Chapter 25). His imaginative ability is chiefly revealed in his invention of what Scout calls 'the biggest ones I ever heard. Among other things, he had been up in a mail plane seventeen times, he had been to Nova Scotia, he had seen an elephant, and his granddaddy was Brigadier General Joe Wheeler and left him his sword' (Chapter 5). This tendency to romantic invention is accounted for by the sadness of Dill's real life; he is unhappy at home and so needs his fantasies for compensation. As Scout explains, he knows the truth but prefers 'his own twilight world where babies slept, waiting to be gathered like morning lilies' (Chapter 14).

Like Jem he loathes cruelty, to such a point that he has to leave the courtroom because the prosecuting attorney's way of speaking to Tom makes him cry. As he says to Scout: '"It made me sick, plain sick"' (Chapter 19). His ultimate reaction to evil is, however, more despairing than Jem's. Where Jem discusses with his father possible means of reforming the legal system, Dill abandons hope and decides the only career for him is as a clown. To him the world is so ugly and unreasonable, and the chance of improving it so impossible, that all one can do is laugh: '"There ain't one thing in this world I can do about folks except laugh, so I'm gonna join the circus and laugh my head off"' (Chapter 22). At first reading this may seem comic, but in fact it is very sad, just as Dill himself is a pathetic character, in spite of all his lively imagination, funny exaggerations and enthusiasm for adventure.

The Ewell family

The Ewells are Atticus's chief opponents in his fight for racial justice, and they belong right at the bottom of the white social scale. Even Atticus, who is the most tolerant of men, describes them as 'absolute trash' (Chapter 12).

Our first introduction to the Ewell family occurs during Scout's first day at school, when the teacher notices a louse in one boy's hair. The boy is Burris Ewell, 'the filthiest human being I had ever seen' (Chapter 3). His behaviour matches his appearance, he slouches rudely out of the classroom after having deliberately reduced the teacher to tears by his foul language. '"Report and be damned to ye! Ain't no snot-nosed slut of a schoolteacher ever born c'n make me do nothin'!"' As we learn more about his family background we come to understand his behaviour. The Ewells live in a filthy shack, surrounded by garbage; the children are dirty, illiterate and diseased. Bob Ewell, the father, is responsible for this state of affairs. His wife is dead; he never works; the sole means of support for his family is relief cheques from the Government, and these he spends on whisky for himself. When he gives evidence in court he is arrogant, ignorant and foul-mouthed. He shows no real concern for his daughter, and can see no reason why he might have been expected to call a doctor for her at the time of the alleged rape. In almost every word he speaks he reveals his crude racial prejudice, even complaining that the 'nigger nest' near his house devalues his property. The readers already know that the black community houses are clean, neat and orderly, in contrast to his own. After the trial he shows his mean, cowardly spirit by attempting revenge only on those unable to resist. At Atticus himself he dares only to spit, and he tries to break into Judge Taylor's house only when he thinks it is empty; but he is brave enough to pester Helen Robinson, whose position as a black woman makes it impossible for her to retaliate, and to attack two young children in the dark.

Mayella Ewell, Bob's eldest daughter, is a different case. In spite of her hopeless home circumstances she makes efforts to look after her younger brothers and sisters, and tries to keep herself clean. No one except Tom Robinson has ever treated her decently; her father gives her no help at all with the family and when Atticus speaks to her in court with ordinary politeness she thinks he must be making fun of her. She has no friends and no opportunity of making friends. In these circumstances it is understandable that she is driven by desperation to make sexual advances to Tom. As Atticus puts it, in doing so '"... she has committed no crime, she has merely broken a rigid and time-honoured code of our society... She knew full well the enormity of her offence, but because her desires were stronger than the code she was breaking, she persisted in breaking it"' (Chapter 20). Atticus pities her, because she is the victim not only of her father but also of the intolerance and prejudice of her society. She lies in court, as her father does, but her crime is much less than his.

The Cunningham family

The Cunninghams, like the Ewells, are poor whites, but their poverty is decent and honourable. They all work hard; they pay their debts, and are capable of loyalty and gratitude.

Their poverty is first revealed to us by the appearance of little Walter Cunningham on Scout's first day at school; he has no shoes or lunch and malnutrition has made him much smaller than Scout even though he is by several years the older of the two. He is backward educationally, because his father has needed his help on the farm, and so has been unable to keep him at school. Atticus has explained earlier to the children that the Cunninghams' poverty is the result of the Depression, and not their own fault. Even in their extreme poverty they are scrupulous in paying debts; when Walter Cunningham has no money to give Atticus in return for legal advice he gives him vegetable produce and firewood instead. Unlike the Ewells the Cunninghams are too proud to accept charity, in the form of either government relief cheques or church baskets from the rich. Atticus tells the children 'the Cunninghams hadn't taken anything from or off anybody since they migrated to the New World' (Chapter 23).

Like the white community in general and the poor whites in particular, the Cunninghams are racially prejudiced. It is Walter Cunningham who leads the lynch mob to the jail before Tom's trial. However, Scout's innocent attempt to make friendly conversation with him is sufficient to make him remember his debt of gratitude to Atticus, and he calls off the mob. After that it is a Cunningham on the jury who supports Atticus and so delays the verdict, because, as Atticus explains, 'once you had earned their respect they were for you tooth and nail' (Chapter 23).

Harper Lee's presentation of the Cunninghams does not make them attractive, but she shows they deserve some respect. She makes clear their ignorance, prejudice and capacity for racial violence, but finds some excuse for these failings in the poverty of their background. Their hard work, determination and independence must evoke some admiration.

The Radley family

The Radley house is the chief focus of interest for Jem and Scout in Part One of the novel. For Harper Lee it provides an example of a variety of social evils: pride, lack of love, isolation in the community, and even religious bigotry. The Radleys never mix with their neighbours; the door of their house is kept shut. Even though the father is reputedly 'so upright that he took the word of God as his only law' (Chapter 1), he never attends church with the rest of the community. The younger son, Arthur, is sacrificed to the cold hearts and family pride of his parents and elder brother.

Arthur Radley, as Miss Maudie remembers him, was once a pleasant boy who always 'spoke as nicely as he knew how'' (Chapter 5). As a teenager he became involved with a gang of Cunningham boys. They drove a car the wrong way round the square and mischievously locked up the officer who tried to arrest them. The other boys are punished in a way which ultimately benefits them: the judge sends them to a state school where they learn useful trades. Mr Radley is too proud to allow his son to be treated in the same way as the poor white Cunninghams. Because of the privileged social position of the Radleys Arthur is excused formal punishment and sent home to his father, who sentences him privately to a lifetime of solitary confinement. He gains the reputation of a dangerous lunatic, but in fact, as Jem and Scout discover, he is only simple-minded, childlike and sweet-natured. He understands the children, gives them the sort of presents they like, and finally saves their lives. In the end, however, he returns to his lonely house, since after the long years of solitude he is too shy to associate with other human beings. It is implied, too, that the long confinement has so weakened his health that he has not long to live. As Miss Maudie says when Scout asks her about the Radleys, '"that is a sad house"' (Chapter 5).

The white ladies

The white ladies of Maycomb form a circle of their own. Not only are they a menace to Scout, who dreads forcible integration into their way of life, but they act as mouthpieces for the narrow-minded prejudice of the white community as a whole. They love to gossip, to congratulate themselves on their own high status and Christian virtue, and to look down upon the blacks. The most prominent among them are Miss Stephanie Crawford, who has a spiteful tongue, and Mrs Merriweather, who poses as the most devout lady in Maycomb and yet shows herself most unchristian in her attitude to race relations.

The one bright spot in the Maycomb ladies' group is Miss Maudie. Scout and Jem love and respect her. She lets them play in her garden and always takes a friendly interest in their activities, even on the morning after the destruction of all her property in a fire. She has a lively sense of humour and no personal pride; she thinks Jem's snowman funny even though the joke is partly against herself, since the snowman wears her hat and hedge-clippers. Unlike other Maycomb ladies she avoids spiteful gossip and racial prejudice, and her strength of character enables her to shame them into silence when they meanly criticise Atticus at the Missionary Circle tea. It is the existence of a character like Miss Maudie even in the white ladies' group that makes it seem as if there is hope for Maycomb society. As Scout once tells her, '"You're the very best lady I know"' (Chapter 5).

The black community

Harper Lee gives a very favourable account of the black community. In general it is shown to possess all the virtues which the white community lacks. Black Christianity is expressed in action; the whites merely talk about it. Blacks are humble where whites are proud; hardworking where whites are lazy. (Laziness among whites is not restricted to men like Bob Ewell; Mr Radley also does no work and Aunt Alexandra's husband spends his days lying in a hammock). Harper Lee frequently contrasts black and white ways of life, usually to the advantage of the blacks. Of First Purchase Church she says: 'Negroes worshipped in it on Sundays and white men gambled in it on weekdays' (Chapter 12). The description of the filthy Ewell residence is placed beside that of the well-kept Negro settlement: '... their cabins looked neat and snug with pale blue smoke rising from the chimney and doorways glowing amber from the fires inside. There were delicious smells about: chicken, bacon frying crisp as the twilight air' (Chapter 17). Their traditional family life too seems preferable to that of most of the whites. Mrs Merriweather, describing the social system of the African tribe which she plans to convert, believes she is painting a deplorable picture. In fact she gives an impression of admirable warmth and security. As Scout reports, 'I learned more about the poor Mrunas' social life from listening to Mrs Merriweather: they had so little sense of family that the whole tribe was one big family. A child had as many fathers as there were men in the community, as many mothers as there were women' (Chapter 27). Dill, Arthur and Mayella would be glad of a chance to live in such a society.

Two black individuals are given prominence in the novel: Tom and Cal. Both are admirable. Tom is kind, generous, courteous and intelligent. He refuses to accept payment for the work he does for Mayella Ewell, because he pities her hard life and admires her efforts to bring up her brothers and sisters. His natural sense of decency makes him unwilling to repeat in court the foul language he heard Bob Ewell use to Mayella. His tact and intelligence enable him to avoid accusing Mayella directly of lying; instead he says she must be 'mistaken in her mind'. Cal, too, is an excellent person. She brings up the children lovingly but firmly, correcting them when they do wrong, comforting them when they are sad, and entertaining them, especially Scout, when they are bored or lonely. Atticus relies on her to run his household and guide his children to do right.

In some respects the presentation of the black community may be considered unrealistic. In the whole novel there is only one character, Lula, who expresses resentment and hostility towards whites. Moreover, there seem to be no bad characters in the black community. As Atticus says in court, 'You know the truth, and the truth is this: some Negroes lie, some Negroes are immoral, some Negro men are not to be trusted around women – black or white. But this is a truth that applies to the whole human race and to no particular race of men' (Chapter 20). All races include some bad characters, and it might be suggested that the black people in this novel seem too good to be true. However, as one of the main objects of the book is to combat prejudice, readers may feel Harper Lee's technique is justified.

Language, imagery and irony

Language

Scout and Jem love words. When Jem offers Miss Maudie some chewing-gum he is charmed by her answer: '". . . she said no thanks, that—chewing gum cleaved to her palate and rendered her speechless . . . . Doesn't that sound nice?"' (Chapter 7). Harper Lee loves words too, and part of the pleasure of reading her novel comes from the range and variety of language used.

All through the book variations in language matter. Scout as narrator is very sensitive to different manners of speech. When Cal uses black grammar rather than white standard English Scout notices at once: '"Cal . . . why do you talk nigger-talk to the—to your folks when you know it's not right?"' (Chapter 12). The different communities, black, white and poor white, are differentiated by their speech. Moreover, the whites' attitude to race is indicated by their choice of terms for referring to the blacks, either as niggers, Negroes, darkies or coloured folks. Language is also used as a means of characterisation. Bob Ewell, for instance, is foul-mouthed and has to be reproved by Judge Taylor for using indecent language in court. Atticus, on the contrary, is rather formal in speech, and this is part of his charm, as there is often an amusing incongruity between style and subject. When Scout makes a bargain with him and prepares to spit, according to Maycomb tradition, to confirm the agreement, he remarks drily: '"We'll consider it sealed without the usual formality"' (Chapter 3). This is comic because of the contrast between the crude action of spitting and the dignified words used to refer to it. It must be realised, however, that Atticus is not a pompous man who uses inflated language all the time to show his own importance. He uses it ironically, and only in appropriate contexts. At moments of crisis he talks to the children in a simple, straightforward way. Among other characters, too, the shifts from one stylistic level to another are used to good effect. When Uncle Jack has punished Scout for fighting Francis their conversation runs as follows: *Uncle Jack:* '"Such conduct as yours required little understanding. It was obstreperous, disorderly, and abusive—"' *Scout:* '"You gonna give me a chance to tell you? I don't mean to sass you, I'm just tryin' to tell you."' (Chapter 9). The humorous effect here comes from the contrast between Uncle Jack's formality and Scout's casual, slangy style.

Finally it should be remembered that though this book is written from a child's point of view, it is not written in a child's language. Scout's point of view has many advantages for the author—it provides opportunities for irony, humour and clarity of moral vision—but to use the restricted vocabulary and grammatical range of a six-year-old would limit Harper Lee's possibilities of expression too much. She makes it clear, therefore, that the book is written by the adult Scout, looking back and recreating her childhood experience. Often she specifically contrasts her adult understanding with the ignorance of childhood, as at the end of Chapter 9, when she is caught listening to her father's conversation with her uncle, and remarks: '...it was not until many years later that I realised he wanted me to hear every word he said'.

Irony

Irony is a subtle technique which depends for its effect on the reader's perception of some sort of incongruity, either between surface meaning and underlying meaning or between words and reality. The incongruity may be obvious at first glance, or it may become apparent only on a second or third reading. It can take various forms.

In its simplest form irony is a kind of sarcasm in which the writer expects the reader to perceive a disparity between what is said and what is meant. Harper Lee often uses this technique in her narration for humorous effect, as in her description of the house at Finch's Landing. 'The internal arrangements of the Finch house were indicative of Simon's guilelessness, and the absolute trust with which he regarded his offspring' (Chapter 9). Immediately afterwards she gives details demonstrating that Simon was extremely guileful and did not trust his children at all, so the readers can detect the irony at once. Another example is to be found in the name of the villain, Bob Ewell. He is called Robert E. Lee Ewell, after the Confederate General acknowledged by both sides in the Civil War to be one of the most upright and honourable men of his time. Here the incongruity is between the admirable character of General Lee and the deplorable character of his namesake.

Another simple form of irony in this novel is the irony of circumstance, often used by the author for comic effect. For instance, when Atticus, in order to please his sister, is trying to teach the children pride and aristocratic behaviour, Scout happens to behave in the middle of his speech in a thoroughly unladylike way. '"Your aunt has asked me to try and impress upon you and Jean Louise that you are not from run-of-the-mill people, that you are the product of several generations' gentle breeding—" Atticus paused, watching me locate an elusive redbug on my leg. "Gentle breeding," he continued, when I had found and scratched it....' (Chapter 13). The incongruity here is between the subject of Atticus's speech and the quality of the action in which Scout is engaged at the very moment he speaks it.

A more complex and serious use of irony occurs when the words spoken by characters are at variance with the realities of the situation as the readers know it. In Scout's class, for instance, the teacher tells the children, during a lesson on Current Events: '"Over here we don't believe in persecuting anybody. Persecution comes from people who are prejudiced"' (Chapter 26). She is talking about Hitler, and her words are ironic because the readers know very well that a Maycomb citizen, Tom Robinson, has just been subjected to prejudice and persecution in an extreme form. The ironic point is made explicit two pages later when Scout asks her brother: '"Jem, how can you hate Hitler so bad, an' then turn around and be ugly about folks right at home?"' Another example of disparity between words and facts occurs in the account of the Missionary Circle tea. The white ladies, confident of their own Christian virtue, kindly announce their intention of reforming and forgiving the black community, especially Helen Robinson. The readers are aware that in reality it is the white ladies themselves who are in need of reform and forgiveness from the very people they despise.

Finally, some degree of irony is inevitably involved in the use of Scout as narrator, since at times there is bound to be disparity between what she, as an inexperienced child, understands and what we, as adult readers, understand. One such occasion is when she hears her father and aunt discussing an unnamed female, whom they refer to as 'her'. At first Scout is worried that she herself is 'her', but after listening a bit longer she stops worrying because she decides that 'her' is Cal. The readers know better, and smile at Scout's naïvety (Chapter 14).

The ironic technique is used frequently in this novel, and for a variety of purposes. It can be comic, as in the case of Scout's childish misapprehensions; it can intensify moral insight, as in the case of Bob Ewell's name, and it can arouse emotional response, as in the case of the Missionary ladies' attitudes, which provoke our contempt and indignation.

Imagery

Scout has a great admiration for imagination. She loves Dill partly for his ability to dream and invent, and she herself displays considerable imaginative power in her use of imagery. She seems to think naturally in images, and this helps to make her narrative style lively. Describing the boring personality of her cousin Francis, for instance, she says: 'Talking to Francis gave me the sensation of settling to the bottom of the ocean' (Chapter 9). Imagistic comparisons are always springing to her mind. As she watches Miss Maudie's fire, and sees the black window frames outlined in the orange flames, she says:'"Jem, it looks like a pumpkin"' (Chapter 8). Her visual images are particularly striking, but she also captures sounds, smells and sensations. Maycomb ladies in the summer evenings remind her of 'soft tea-cakes with frostings of sweat and talcum' (Chapter 1). Mrs Dubose's breathing mouth reminds her of a clam-hole at low tide, and she notices that occasionally 'it would say, "Pt," like some viscous substance coming to a boil' (Chapter 11). Her images communicate meaning very clearly and directly, as they are usually drawn from concrete everyday experience. Her bored classmates are described as 'wriggling like a bucketful of catawba worms' (Chapter 2). When she fears Atticus is getting into difficulties in his own cross-examination of Bob Ewell it seems to her that 'he'd gone frog-sticking without a light' (Chapter 17). Her favourite form of imagery is the simile, but she can also produce vivid metaphors. When Aunt Alexandra embarks on the campaign to make her more ladylike she says: 'I could feel the starched walls of a pink cotton penitentiary closing in on me' (Chapter 14). The use of imagery is an effective feature of Scout's narrative style.

One aspect of the imagery which comes directly from Harper Lee, rather than Scout, is the symbolism implied in the title. Mockingbirds are first mentioned in the story when Atticus gives the children guns and warns them that '"it's a sin to kill a mockingbird"' (Chapter 10). Miss Maudie explains that this is because mockingbirds do no damage to crops—'"... they don't do one thing but sing their hearts out for us"'. On one level, therefore, mockingbirds are a symbol of innocence, and Tom Robinson is a sort of mockingbird. He has done no harm; in fact he has served the white community with his labour just as the mockingbird serves humanity with its song. After Tom's death Mr Underwood's editorial in the *Maycomb Tribune* makes the parallel explicit. 'He likened Tom's death to the senseless slaughter of songbirds by hunters and children' (Chapter 25). Arthur Radley, whose suffering in some respects parallels Tom's, is another mockingbird. When Atticus tries to explain to Scout why Arthur must be spared the publicity which would result from informing the community of his part in the children's escape, she understands at once: '"Well, it'd be sort of like shootin' a mockingbird, wouldn't it?"' (Chapter 30).

Innocence is not the only meaning of the mockingbird symbol. Mockingbirds are also used as symbols of happiness and security, symbols of a world without fear or evil. When the mockingbirds fall silent it is a sign that the situation is ugly and dangerous. When the rabid dog is approaching the house: 'The trees were still, the mockingbirds were silent, the carpenters at Miss Maudie's house had vanished' (Chapter 10). In the courtroom at Tom's trial, even though the day is hot, the atmosphere reminds Scout of that earlier occasion; it was 'exactly the same as a cold February morning when the mockingbirds were still and the carpenters had stopped hammering on Miss Maudie's new house' (Chapter 21). The implication here is that the members of the jury who are about to re-enter the courtroom with their verdict are as mad and vicious as the rabid dog.

The fullest description of mockingbirds comes towards the end of the book, when Scout and Jem are walking to the pageant. 'High above us in the darkness a solitary mocker poured out his repertoire in blissful unawareness of whose tree he sat in, plunging from the shrill kee, kee of the sunflower bird to the irascible qua-ack of a blue jay, to the sad lament of Poor Will, Poor Will, Poor Will' (Chapter 28). The tree in which the bird sits is the tree in the Radley garden, and this is fitting, since Arthur Radley is himself a sort of mockingbird. There is also a further suggestion here. The mockingbird imitates the songs of different birds—the blue jay, the sunflower bird and the whippoorwill. It is doing, in a sense, exactly what Atticus has told the children that they should try to do: to stand in other people's shoes. The mockingbird is more flexible than human beings; it constantly takes the part of other birds.

Mockingbirds are used, therefore, in a variety of ways as symbols of goodness in this novel. The title *To Kill a Mockingbird* means 'to destroy innocence and happiness'. It is no accident, perhaps, that the best human being in the story is given the name of a bird—Finch.

Part 4

Hints for study

WHEN PREPARING a literary text for an examination it is helpful to remember that examination questions are usually concentrated in certain predictable areas. In the case of novels these areas include interpretation of themes, analysis of characters, analysis of structure, use of setting and use of language. Suggestions on how to approach these areas follow.

Themes

The themes of a novel are the main ideas which the author has presented. On first reading you should decide what ideas you think the writer is trying to convey, what points have received special emphasis, and what conclusions about life can be drawn from the novel as a whole.

In the case of *To Kill a Mockingbird* a useful way to begin is to decide what is the main or climactic event in the book, as this may help to identify the author's chief area of concern. The high point in the action is clearly the trial of Tom Robinson, so it seems likely that racial prejudice is the main theme. However, the Robinson case becomes prominent only in Part Two. In Part One the racial issue is not dominant, so though it is obviously a major part of the central theme it may not be the whole theme. At this point you should find what other concepts are stressed, especially in Part One, Harper Lee gives some help here by her technique of repeating key ideas several times. Among these recurrent ideas are the question of social status, the suggestion that we should stand in each other's shoes, and of course the references to mockingbirds. By careful consideration of such points you can arrive at a broad, comprehensive definition of the novel's major concern. Harper Lee is troubled by the failure of the human race to live together in peace and friendship. She wants to analyse the forces dividing man from man. A key phrase summing up her concern is provided by Mr Raymond when he speaks of 'the simple hell people give other people' (Chapter 20).

After deciding that Harper Lee is troubled by the 'hell people give other people', you should go on to make a systematic analysis of the sorts of hell described in the novel. At least three varieties can be found: the hell of family life; the hell of social stratification, and the hell of racialism. Mr Radley, Bob Ewell, Dill's mother and old Simon Finch provide various hells for their children. The hell people give each other by social snobbery affects the lower ranks of society. The Ewells are ostracised by the white community so that Mayella, who has the potential for leading a decent life, has no friends at all. Little Walter Cunningham is not allowed to associate with the Finch children because of Aunt Alexandra's class-consciousness. The hell people give each other through racial prejudice is the clearest of all. Black people are deprived of educational, financial and professional opportunities, and in Tom's case even of life itself. His is the most extreme example of the hell people give each other, and this is why it is given such prominence in Part Two.

After locating and analysing the major theme you should go on to find what other ideas are worth exploring. In *To Kill a Mockingbird* it is clear that Harper Lee is interested in children. The narrator is a child; her closest companions are children; the novel spans several years and thus shows how the children grow and develop. Again you should approach the matter systematically, dividing the idea of childhood up into the various aspects with which the author is concerned.

First decide what Harper Lee thinks of children in general. You will soon realise that she holds them in high respect. Key phrases which help define her attitude are to be found in Atticus's suggestion that '"We need a police force of children"' (Chapter 16), and his reaction after the verdict against Tom, '"seems that only children weep"' (Chapter 22). In Harper Lee's eyes children are good and innocent, not just in the narrow sense, as when Scout does not understand the words 'whore-lady', but in that they are literally incapable of comprehending adult prejudices and cruelties. She feels, too, that children have naturally eager, inquiring minds. They can learn a lot, and they can be easily influenced. Jem and Scout are growing up as decent human beings because they have their father's example to follow.

After deciding what Harper Lee feels are the essential qualities of childhood you should investigate the ways in which she thinks children develop. Boys like Jem become moody, selfconscious and sensitive as they approach adolescence. Girls like Scout have to adapt gradually to the feminine role. Both have to suffer as they grow. Jem, as the older and more thoughtful, is always ahead of Scout in maturity of understanding. As the two develop Harper Lee shows what lessons she considers most valuable as preparation for adult life. The children have to learn self-control, tolerance, respect for the rights of others, and courage to withstand shame, defeat and failure. They absorb these lessons in Part One, and get an opportunity to put them into practice in Part Two.

The two main themes outlined above can be subdivided for fuller analysis. The question of how men mistreat each other can be considered under a variety of headings: family life; loneliness; racialism; snobbery. The presentation of childhood can also be considered from various points of view; as a process of development; as a presentation of the ideas of innocence in conflict with experience; as a means of conveying moral ideas, or simply as a realistic description of a particular stage in human growth. You should practise looking at themes from as many angles as possible, so as to be prepared for a variety of approaches in the examination.

Sample questions on theme

1. Write an essay on Harper Lee's presentation of *one* of the following topics: race relations; family life; childhood; social snobbery.

2. What are the major faults which Harper Lee finds in Maycomb society?

3. How far is Harper Lee optimistic about the possibility of an improvement in human relations?

. 4. What is the relevance of the title *To Kill a Mockingbird* to the plot of the novel?

5. At the end of the novel Scout claims that there is not much left for herself and Jem to learn. What lessons has she absorbed in the course of the novel?

6. How does the use of a child narrator influence our response to *To Kill a Mockingbird*?

Characterisation

Where characterisation is concerned the novelist's task is to create interesting and convincing human beings whose adventures we shall want to follow. The student's task is to analyse the nature, psychology and motivation of the characters, so as to understand what sort of people they are, why they act as they do, and how their conduct should be judged in the context of the novel. It is necessary to form a clear idea of the nature of all the prominent major and minor characters, and to memorise details which will illustrate and support your analysis.

The first step is to collect material for an analysis of each character. Material can be found in a variety of areas. First, character is revealed in action, not only major actions such as Atticus's defence of Tom, but also minor actions, trivial in themselves but significant in their contribution to the total picture. In the case of Miss Maudie, for instance, her friendliness, understanding of children and lack of pride are revealed by the way in which she allows Scout to make a close inspection of her false teeth. 'With a click of her tongue she thrust out her bridgework, a gesture of cordiality that cemented our friendship' (Chapter 5). Second, character is revealed by manner of speech. Atticus is invariably polite and usually formal; Bob Ewell is always vulgar and often indecent.

Third, we can rely to some extent on the accounts characters give of each other, though here we must be sure the character speaking can be trusted. Miss Maudie's descriptions of Atticus, for example, are perfectly reliable. Fourth, characters often describe themselves, though here again we have to be cautious. Some characters are truthful; others flatter themselves. Atticus is honest; when he says he tries to love everybody he can be believed because his actions prove it. But when Mrs Merriweather explains what a good Christian she is we note this only as an example of her pride and self-deception, since her racialist attitudes show she is not Christian at all. A fifth source of material for character analysis is family and social background. In the case of Dill, for example, the tendency to fantasise can be explained by his unhappy home. Finally, a useful short cut to character analysis may be found in imagery. In the trial scene, for example, Bob Ewell is compared to a little bantam cock and his daughter to a cat with a twitchy tail. The implications of these similes are worth consideration.

After completing analysis of all the main characters you should study the ways in which they are used to contribute to the themes of the novel. Atticus, for instance, is used as a model for the ideal of truly civilised behaviour. Mr Raymond provides a lesson in the irrationality of racial prejudice. Mrs Dubose shows what courage really means.

Finally, when the characters have been analysed and the author's purpose in presenting them investigated, you can judge the success of the characterisation as a whole. Do the characters seem realistic? In assessing realism it is useful to notice whether major characters show any change or development, since in real life people are always being altered, however slightly, by experience. At the same time you should check whether characters seem consistent. If, for instance, Miss Maudie suddenly behaved rudely to a black person, this would not fit in with her character, and so would seem unconvincing. Also, in real life there are no perfectly good or bad people. Everyone possesses a mixture of good and bad qualities. Check, therefore, to see whether any characters seem too good or bad to be true.

In reviewing characterisation before the examination it is helpful to find a few key phrases which seem to sum up individuals. Miss Maudie's description of Atticus as 'civilized in his heart' is an example of this.

Sample questions on character

1. Mr Raymond tells Scout: 'Your pa's not a run-of-the-mill man'. Illustrate the truth of this statement from the plot of the novel.

2. Choose *two* of the following characters and show what they contribute to the novel as a whole: Miss Maudie; Mrs Dubose; Bob Ewell; Dill Harris.

3. Trace the development in the character of *either* Jem *or* Scout through the course of the novel.

4. Write an essay on Harper Lee's presentation of the black characters in *To Kill a Mockingbird*.

Structure

Analysis of a novel's structure involves examination of the way in which an author has organised his material. The basic question is whether the novel seems well planned, and the chief criterion for good planning is unity of design. A novel is said to be well unified when all the episodes can be seen to be relevant. Another aspect of structure is the question of whether the events are arranged in such a way as to hold the reader's interest and build up to a satisfying climax.

In the case of *To Kill a Mockingbird* the problem of unity is particularly interesting, because the connection between Parts One and Two is not immediately obvious. Part Two is well unified in itself, since it is almost all concerned with the Robinson trial. Part One, however, contains a wide variety of episodes. The problem here is to trace what relevance the episodes in Part One have to the main topic of Part Two. In the case of the account of Scout's first day at school, for instance, Harper Lee uses the episode to introduce various matters necessary as preparation for the events of Part Two. She introduces the Ewells and the Cunninghams, and gives some idea of the special characteristics of Southern culture in general and Maycomb society in particular. All this background detail prepares the reader for the events of Part Two.

As regards manipulation of climax the questions to be asked concern the handling of both major and minor points of excitement. The major climax of the novel is the trial. You should ask yourself whether you experience any decline of interest after the trial is over. Do the final chapters seem anti-climactic? If not, how does Harper Lee succeed in sustaining interest? For minor climaxes you should look closely at the ways in which individual chapters are ended. Do they finish on a note which makes you eager to read on? Sometimes Harper Lee ends a chapter on a sensational note, as in the case of Chapter 22, which ends with Bob Ewell spitting in Atticus's face. Sometimes there is a hint of something exciting to come, as in the case of Chapter 27, which ends as Jem and Scout set out for the pageant: 'Thus began our longest journey together'.

Sample questions on structure

---

1. Jem claims in Chapter 1 that the story begins in the summer when Dill first arrived. Show whether you agree or disagree with him.

2. Explain what any *one* of the following episodes contributes to the novel as a whole: the shooting of the rabid dog; the visit to Cal's church; the children's encounter with Mrs Dubose.

Setting

The setting of a novel is its position in time and space. *To Kill a Mockingbird* is set in Alabama in the 1930s, and both the geographical and the historical location help us to interpret the novel. In this section some suggestions are made on ways of analysing the various uses of setting.

First, setting can reveal character. The description of the Ewell house shows the lazy irresponsibility of Bob Ewell's character; the geraniums in the yard show Mayella's desire to live a better life. The Radley house, with its permanently closed doors and shutters, reflects the cold and unfriendly character of its owner. The peculiar architecture of Finch's Landing reveals the meanness of its builder, Simon Finch.

As well as revealing individual character, setting can help us to form balanced moral judgements. The behaviour of Maycomb residents is conditioned by their background, the narrow provincialism of their lives and the harshness of the economic circumstances. Understanding of the setting will prevent us from judging Maycomb characters too harshly, even though we condemn their racial prejudice. Similarly, knowledge of the physical conditions in which Mayella lives helps us to pity rather than blame her. The pressures of environment should always be taken into account when judging behaviour.

A further function of setting is the creation of atmosphere. The Radley house, with its rotting roof and neglected garden, communicates the sadness appropriate to Arthur's situation. The silence and stillness of the February day when the rabid dog appears increase our sense of suspense. The brightness of the Negro cemetery gives a sense of the happy, healthy quality of black culture. Description of setting can thus be used very effectively to evoke emotional response.

In preparing this topic for examinations the first step should be to make a list of all the settings described in the book, from Maycomb City in general to individual buildings such as First Purchase Church. For a proper appreciation of an author's use of setting it is necessary to observe detail closely. A general impression is not enough, since a good novelist will make every detail count.

Sample questions on setting

---

1. How does the description of the Ewell house contribute to our understanding of the Ewell family's role in the novel?

2. How is our response to the black community affected by the descriptions of their church, cemetery, and Quarters?

3. What aspects of small-town life does Harper Lee show which influence the behaviour of the inhabitants?

Language

To Kill a Mockingbird is written in modern American English, and the style is basically informal, since the narrator is a child. The author, however, does not try to keep within the limits of a child's vocabulary or powers of expression. A wide range of language is used in the novel, and in studying it the first step should be to identify the various levels of style used. This is easy, since the variations in language correspond to the divisions in social class. The black dialect differs from the white; the rich whites speak more grammatically than the poor whites; highly educated characters like Atticus and his brother Jack speak more elegantly than town officials like Heck Tate.

After listing the varieties of language to be found in the novel you should analyse the author's purpose in using them. First, differences in social class and educational status are revealed by differing use of language. Secondly, individual character is often revealed by distinctive style of speech (as in the cases of Atticus and Bob Ewell). Thirdly, attitudes to moral issues can often be detected by analysis of language, even when the characters speaking belong to the same social class and might therefore be expected to use identical words. You could, for instance, check the terms used by different rich white individuals to refer to the blacks—some say nigger, some say darky, some say Negro, some say coloured persons—and take the word they choose as an indication of their racial attitude. A minor example of the same type of variation in usage is to be found in the name used by various characters for the narrator. Friends call her Scout; enemies call her Jean Louise.

One further function of the language used in this novel is the creation of atmosphere. All the characters, even the highly educated Atticus, use distinctive Southern dialect expressions such as 'You all'. Many names used for local fruits and vegetables are also distinctively Southern. It is hard for foreign students to appreciate this technique, but its effect is to create a vivid sense of the Southern environment.

Sample questions on language

---

1. Show how language is used to indicate character in *To Kill a Mockingbird*.

2. How are varieties of social status indicated by speech in *To Kill a Mockingbird*?

Extra questions

Often examination questions take the form of quotations whose meaning and relevance you are asked to discuss. The following are typical examples of the sort of quotation which might be selected.

1. '"Simply because we were licked a hundred years before we started is no reason for us not to try to win"' (Atticus).

2. '"The one thing that doesn't abide by majority rule is a person's conscience"' (Atticus).

Organisation of essays

When choosing which question to answer in an examination paper you should not rush. Make sure you have enough material to write not just one paragraph but five or six. Make sure, too, that you plan the arrangement of your material before you start writing, so that you get your ideas on to the paper in the most logical and effective order.

Having selected your question, you should first make a quick list on a piece of rough paper of the points which you want to include in your answer. If, for instance, you are writing about the character of Dill, your list might include items like his small size, his unhappy home life, his engagement to Scout, his desire for a baby, his interest in Arthur Radley, his crying in court, his powers of invention and his wish to be a clown. When your list is complete read it through and cross out anything that on consideration seems irrelevant. When the list seems complete and relevant you should arrange your points in a logical order. If you have remembered several different occasions when Dill tells lies (for instance, saying his father has a beard; that Jem lost his trousers playing strip poker; that he joined a circus when he ran away from home), put them all together in a group. If various different items on your list all seem to illustrate a single basic idea (for example, Dill's loneliness and insecurity), put them together, too.

At this stage you should be ready to start writing. Try to make your opening sentence interesting, one that will catch the attention of the examiner. Short sentences are often best from this point of view. If you can remember a short, relevant quotation it will provide a lively start. In the case of Dill you might remember Scout's description of him as a 'pocket Merlin', and use it in the first sentence. In general, the opening paragraph of your essay should be used to introduce the topic you are discussing. It is often a good idea to give a sort of summary of what you intend to say in the essay, listing the main points you intend to cover.

In the middle part of the essay you should develop your main points. Each separate paragraph should contain one main idea, illustrated by two or three examples or illustrations from the text. (For instance, if the paragraph concerns Dill's habit of lying, you should give at least two examples of occasions when he tells lies.)

Your last paragraph should provide a conclusion, or general summing-up of your ideas on the topic. If, for instance, you find that the main tendency of your answer seems to demonstrate that Dill is a good but unfortunate character, you could conclude by stating that all the evidence goes to show that Dill is a nice person, but not as lucky as Jem and Scout in his family background.

In general it is not necessary to write very long essays in examinations. Six or seven paragraphs of reasonable length are usually enough. When reading through your answer before handing it in you should check to make sure that each paragraph deals with a distinct aspect of the topic, and that you have not repeated yourself.

In preparing for the examination it is always useful to try to memorise a few quotations, though in the case of novels this is harder than it is with poetry or drama. It is usually possible, however, to pick out a few short key phrases (for example, Miss Maudie's description of Atticus as 'civilized in his heart'). Often images are easy to remember (an example is Scout's idea that Aunt Alexandra fits into Maycomb society 'like a hand into a glove'). Try to select one key phrase illustrating each major character, one key phrase summing up the nature of the social background, and one key phrase on each of the major themes. A short quotation makes a very effective final sentence, as well as a good opening.

Model answers

1. Write an essay on Harper Lee's presentation of the theme of family life in *To Kill a Mockingbird*

One of the most pathetic moments in *To Kill a Mockingbird* is when Dill, having run away from home, tells Scout that he did so because his mother and new stepfather simply did not need him. They were not cruel to him; they gave him presents and told him to enjoy himself, but he realised that they did not really want him. This incident reveals Harper Lee's deep concern with failure in family life. She believes it is essential for children to grow up in an atmosphere of love and security. Through the novel she provides many examples of family life, both good and bad, and strongly emphasises the unhappy results of parental failure to care properly for children.

The Radley family provides an extreme example of parental failure. The son, Arthur Radley, gets involved in teenage mischief with a gang of local boys. They commit no serious crime, but Arthur's father is so harsh and cruel that he punishes his son by making him a prisoner in the house for the rest of his life. As a result Arthur's physical and mental health suffer, and he comes to be regarded as a crazy monster, nicknamed 'Boo' by the people of the town. Yet from his behaviour to Scout and Jem, giving them presents and finally saving them from Bob Ewell, it is evident that he is good, kind and gentle. His mind seems childlike and undeveloped, but he is obviously sweet-natured. His cruel father has ruined his life; when Arthur visits the Finch house at the end of the book his long confinement has made him so shy that he can scarcely speak and tries to hide in a dark corner of the room.

Dill Harris's family problems are less extreme than Arthur's. His parents are divorced; his mother has remarried, and he can tell that she and his new stepfather are not really interested in him, even though they make him gifts of expensive toys. That is why he runs away from home. He feels the need of a proper family life, and so he proposes marriage to Scout and suggests that they themselves get a baby. A further effect of his unsatisfactory home background is that he is a great liar. He is always telling Jem and Scout impossible stories about his adventures, and can easily invent lies to deceive the grown-ups when the children get into trouble. This power of invention seems to be a way of compensating for his home problems. He prefers the imaginary world he can invent to the real world in which he has to live. He is basically a nice little boy, but he has no grown-ups to rely on. His aunt Rachel, with whom he spends his summer holidays in Maycomb, shows no more genuine affection for him than his mother and stepfather.

Burris and Mayella Ewell provide further examples of the evil effects of lack of proper parental care. Burris comes to school on the first day of term looking filthy and neglected. He is educationally backward for his age. He behaves rudely and aggressively to his teacher. When his father, Bob Ewell, appears later in the book we can see that Burris is simply imitating his father's bad example. The case of his sister Mayella is more pathetic. She would like to lead a decent life; she tries to keep clean, to look after her little brothers and sisters, and even to grow pretty flowers in the garden. But her father gives her no love and no help, and in the end her frustration drives her to folly of the most extreme kind, since it is her actions which are ultimately responsible for Tom Robinson's death. The Ewell children get no care, no protection and no guidance from their father; all he gives them is his bad example, so they have no chance of growing up as decent members of society.

The Finch family is like the Ewell family in being motherless, but there is no other resemblance. Jem and Scout Finch have a perfect family life; their father loves, guides and protects them, and always provides a good example by his own conduct. When they do wrong he corrects them, but he is never too strict or repressive. The children love, respect and trust him. When Scout is miserable she always runs to sit on his knee. She knows he will stay all night by Jem's bed when Jem's elbow is broken. Whatever difficulties the children experience in the course of the book, especially at the time of the trial, they are able to survive them because of their warm, secure and happy family background.

Every description of child-parent relationships in this book tends to demonstrate the vital importance of a good family life. What matters is not money but love. The Radleys are rich but cold, whereas the Cunningham family is poor but united, and does its best for its children. Little Walter Cunningham is dressed in poor but clean clothes; he feels close to his family and in consequence his whole attitude to life is more positive and responsible than that of Burris Ewell. As a whole *To Kill a Mockingbird* is concerned with the need to improve human society, and the examples of the Radley, Harris and Ewell families suggest that the improvement could and should begin at the family level.

---

2. Write an essay on Harper Lee's presentation of the black characters in *To Kill a Mockingbird*.

One of the main themes in *To Kill a Mockingbird* is racial injustice. The major event is the trial and conviction of an innocent black man for the supposed rape of a white girl. Harper Lee uses the novel to attack the racial prejudice which can lead to such injustice. She therefore presents the black community in a very favourable way, showing their sufferings, so the readers will pity them, and their virtues, so they will admire them.

The members of the white community in Maycomb look down on the black community. They consider black people to be stupid, lazy, immoral and incapable of any sort of equality with the whites. The social status of the blacks is as low as possible. They are deprived of educational opportunity, as is shown by the fact that most of the congregation of Cal's church are illiterate. Only the lowest jobs are available to them, as servants or as labourers in the cotton industry, and those jobs are very poorly paid. Moreover, they are the object of a strange sexual suspicion from the whites, who believe that all black men are eager to rape white women. The Missionary Circle ladies complain that no white woman is safe from attack, and describe the blacks as being incapable of 'civilization'. With this background of prejudice Atticus has no hope of winning his case. As he says himself, when the trial comes the jury will automatically believe the white man rather than the black. He is right. Tom is found guilty simply because of racial prejudice. His case is only the most outrageous example in the book of a whole range of instances of intolerance, injustice and cruelty to blacks. Even the way the whites refer to them reveals contempt. They say 'nigger' rather than 'Negro' and 'wool' rather than 'hair'.

While the white population is shown to be mean, unjust and exploitive in its treatment of blacks, the black people themselves are shown to be kind, patient and generous by nature. As a group they always seem to behave well. The First Purchase Church puts its Christianity into practice where the whites do not; the whole black congregation contributes money for the support of the Robinson family. The black spectators at the trial are quiet and patient, and show their instinctive courtesy when they all rise as a sign of respect to Atticus when he leaves the court. Even though they are very poor they send food to his house out of gratitude when the trial is over. Their general attitude to the whites seems extremely patient and unresentful. Only one character, the woman Lula, shows any hostility to the whites, and that is on the occasion when she objects to Cal's taking Jem and Scout to the African church. All the rest of the congregation contradict her and rush to welcome the white children.

The virtues common to the black population as a whole are specially emphasised in the characters of the book's two most prominent black individuals: the Finches' cook, Cal, and Tom Robinson. Cal acts almost like a mother to Jem and Scout; Atticus refers to her as a member of the family. She is kind and loving to the children, and comforts them when they are in trouble. She also teaches them high moral standards, as is clear when she scolds Scout for rudely drawing attention to little Walter Cunningham's low-class eating habits. She is a responsible member of the community, and takes care to warn all the houses in the street when the rabid dog is approaching. Atticus tells his sister that without Cal the Finch household could not survive.

Like Cal, Tom Robinson is shown to be a fine person. He is a thoroughly reliable workman, as his employer, Mr Link Deas, tries to point out at the trial. He is very kind; he helps Mayella Ewell with household tasks and never asks for payment. He is naturally polite, and during the trial is reluctant to repeat the dirty words spoken by Bob Ewell, because there are children present in court. He is a good husband and father, as even the Missionary Circle ladies have to admit. Also, he is intelligent; he avoids the danger of calling a white person a liar by choosing his words carefully, so instead of saying in court that Mayella is lying he says she 'is mistaken in her mind'. His behaviour all through the trial impresses the readers with his dignity, generosity, patience and human decency.

The settings in which the black people live are also used to give a favourable picture of their culture. Their church is a poor building; they cannot even afford to paint the walls, but it is clean, neat and decorated as beautifully as possible. The cemetery outside strikes Scout as a 'happy' place; the graves are carefully tended and the atmosphere is pleasant. The black community's houses, which are segregated from those of the whites, are poor and simple but very well kept, and seem warm and friendly. In general the black people seem to make the best of their surroundings, even though they cannot afford much.

Harper Lee's attitude to the black characters in this book is summed up in a phrase she uses to describe their behaviour as they wait in the court to hear the jury's verdict. She says they stood or sat 'with Biblical patience'. The adjective 'Biblical' conveys the impression that these black people are truly dignified and also deeply religious. It is clear that Harper Lee wants us to respect the blacks as well as pity them. It is noticeable, too, that she has not included any bad characters among them. This might be considered unrealistic, since in any human community there must be some undesirable characters, but it must be understood as a deliberate technique. The author is doing her very best to refute the unreasonable white Southern belief that blacks are immoral and inferior.

---

3. 'Simply because we were licked a hundred years before we started is no reason for us not to try to win' (Atticus). Show the relevance of this statement to the action and characters of *To Kill a Mockingbird*.

In *To Kill a Mockingbird* the good characters *are* licked a hundred years before they start, because the history of the American South is against them. The hero, Atticus Finch, is chosen to act as defence attorney for a black man, Tom Robinson, who is accused of raping a white girl. Atticus has no chance of winning the case, because there is strong racial prejudice in Maycomb County, prejudice whose roots stretch back far into the past. Even so, as Harper Lee believes and Atticus himself says, to struggle for justice is always worth while. She invites us to admire Atticus's courage and perseverance in this hopeless struggle, and at the end of the novel she shows that in this case even defeat has a positive aspect. Atticus was right to try, even though he knew he was defeated before he began.

The story of the novel is a story of defeat for good men. Tom Robinson is a good man; but he is condemned in the minds of the white community before he ever comes to trial. Atticus is a good lawyer, but he knows he is certain to lose Tom's case simply because Tom is black. He has to argue not just against the prosecuting attorney but against the prejudice of the white community as a whole. This prejudice is as old as the history of the American South. It dates back, most of all, to the time of the Civil War of 1861–5, in which the South fought to preserve black slavery, and the North fought to abolish it. The North won; the black people were officially freed, but white Southerners refused to change their attitudes. White Maycomb County inhabitants are still convinced in 1935 that blacks are basically inferior and naturally immoral. The bitterness of Southern defeat in the Civil War is still working in their hearts and inclining them to even greater distrust both of the black community and of the liberal 'Northern' ideas which Atticus stands for. History is against him, and in that sense he is indeed 'licked' a hundred years before he starts. He is licked by the past itself, by the whole history of slavery, Civil War and black/white relationships in the South.

Atticus is licked before he begins, and he knows it, but he still feels he should try. Here he displays a quality which Harper Lee really admires: true courage. This is not the superficial courage of a man with a gun, but the mental fortitude which enables a man to go on fighting for a cause which he knows is hopeless. Atticus goes against his own community for the sake of what he believes to be right; he brings suffering to his family, and he does all this in the knowledge that his sacrifice will not be rewarded by success. Courage is very highly regarded in the Southern cultural tradition, and Harper Lee is concerned here to define exactly what courage involves. To emphasise her point she includes another example, that of Mrs Dubose, an evil-tempered old woman who is dying in great pain. Atticus wants his children to be acquainted with her so that they can learn from her example what courage is. She is dying in agony; she has no hope of defeating her disease, but she is brave enough to struggle for her dignity and self-respect to the end. She does so by deliberately breaking her morphine-addiction so as to die a free woman. Like Atticus she was in a hopeless situation, but she still fought for what she believed to be right.

Mrs Dubose has to fight her drug-addiction right up to the time of her death. It takes repeated efforts, day after day. This is another quality which Harper Lee admires: the ability to persevere, which in her view is a necessary aspect of true courage. Atticus demonstrates this virtue in his behaviour after the trial. At first he seems discouraged by his failure. He retires to bed leaving instructions that he is not to be woken at his usual early hour the next morning. It is as if he does not want to face the new day. However, when the children come down to breakfast the following morning they find their father in his place as usual, ready to encourage them to take an optimistic view of Tom's chances in the appeal court. This is genuine courage, involving not only the willingness to fight against impossible odds, knowing that defeat is a certainty, but to do so again and again without getting discouraged.

In the racial situation of the American South in the 1930s Harper Lee thinks there can be no easy victory for justice. The white community prejudice against the blacks is too strong and too deeply rooted to be changed overnight. This is why the South needs heroes like Atticus, prepared to struggle on and on and able to accept setbacks without despairing. It is also why Harper Lee lays such emphasis on the virtue of courage. Finally, at the end of the novel, she offers a hint of hope. Atticus knew he was licked before he started and yet, as Miss Maudie tries to explain to the children, he was not entirely licked after all. He was defeated in court, but the defeat itself was a kind of victory, since though the jury found Tom guilty it took several hours to arrive at the verdict. Without Atticus it would not have taken as much as a minute. Miss Maudie sees this as progress, a 'baby-step' in the right direction. Without men like Atticus societies like Maycomb, with a weight of tragic history behind them, would make no progress at all.

---

4. Explain what the Dubose episode contributes to the novel as a whole.

The children's encounter with Mrs Dubose takes place at the end of Part One of *To Kill a Mockingbird*. It begins when Jem, enraged by the insults which Mrs Dubose shouts as the children pass her home, deliberately smashes the camellia flowers in her garden. The insults which provoke his action are all directed at Atticus. Mrs Dubose tells the children that their father is 'no better than the niggers and trash he works for'. When Atticus learns what has happened he sends Jem to apologise at once to Mrs Dubose. After that Jem has to go every afternoon after school to read aloud to the old lady. Scout goes too, to keep Jem company. Mrs Dubose goes on insulting the children throughout the reading sessions, which continue for five weeks. Not long afterwards she dies, and Atticus returns from her death-bed to inform the children that she had been a morphine-addict. She used the afternoon reading sessions as a means of breaking her drug-addiction, because she wanted to die 'free'. Atticus asks the children to respect her as 'a great lady', and also, as he says, 'the bravest person I ever knew'. The position of this episode, coming at a climatic spot at the end of Part One, shows that Harper Lee considers it crucial. Its function is to give readers an opportunity to increase their understanding of major themes and characters in the novel.

First, Jem and Scout learn a lot from their association with Mrs Dubose. Jem learns how to control his feelings and keep calm in spite of provocation. During the reading sessions the old lady continues to insult Atticus, but Jem does not react. He also gets an opportunity to practise Southern gentlemanly behaviour. No matter how Mrs Dubose behaves, he has to remember that she is an old lady and therefore must be treated with courtesy and respect. At the same time both children are able to see real courage in action. Mrs Dubose bears her pain and fights her addiction in order to keep her self-respect, even though she knows she is dying. Finally, when Atticus explains about her illness and addiction, Jem and Scout can see how helpful it is to try to 'get into other people's skins', to try to see things from their point of view. To them Mrs Dubose was simply a horrible old woman, but when they understand that she was constantly in agony they can sympathise with her bad temper. This is a lesson in not judging others too harshly. Self-control, true courtesy, true courage and sympathetic tolerance of others are all lessons that Maycomb County needs to learn if tragic cases like that of Tom Robinson are to be prevented.

Secondly, the Dubose episode provides further insight into several major characters. Atticus, in particular, shows his moral excellence as a man and as a father. His behaviour towards Mrs Dubose is most courteous. Though she has publicly insulted him he always greets her in a polite and friendly way. He attends at her death-bed and encourages his children to respect her virtues rather than condemn her faults. In all this he shows himself to be truly a gentleman. He also behaves very well with his children, being both strict and kind. He makes Jem apologise to Mrs Dubose, but comforts Scout when she fears the old lady will shoot her brother.

For the children's characters, too, this episode is very illuminating. We see Jem's gradual progress towards maturity, as he learns self-discipline; we see Scout's warm heart and instinctive courage. Though she is terrified of Mrs Dubose her loyalty to her brother makes her accompany him to every reading session, even though she is not officially included in the punishment. At the same time we see Jem's kindness to his sister, for the trouble with Mrs Dubose begins on the day when the children go to the shops to spend Jem's birthday money, which he uses to get two presents, one for himself and one for Scout. In general, the Dubose episode increases our sympathy and admiration for all three members of the Finch family.

This episode also reveals the attitudes of the whites in Maycomb towards race relations. Mrs Dubose is a typical white Maycomb lady in that she looks down on black people, whom she invariably refers to as 'niggers'. One of her main criticisms of Atticus is that he has disgraced himself by taking on the Robinson case. Because she is in constant pain and therefore rather violent in temper, she puts very frankly into words prejudices which other Maycomb residents do not express quite so openly. Through her we understand the deep-seated intolerance of Maycomb society. At the same time, in the account of her black maid Jessie, we see the admirable qualities of the very people whom she despises. Mrs Dubose is entirely dependent on Jessie's faithful service. She speaks contemptuously of 'niggers', but relies on a 'nigger' for her very existence. In this way the Dubose episode provides insight into the social background of Maycomb, thus helping to prepare us for the climax of the book, that is, the trial of Tom Robinson.

The Dubose episode provides a suitable climax for the first part of *To Kill a Mockingbird* because it contains so much useful material on theme, character and social background. At the end of the book, when Scout stands on the Radley porch recalling all the major events of the past two years, the name of Mrs Dubose comes to her mind.

Part 5

Suggestions for further reading

The text

To Kill a Mockingbird, Lippincott, Philadelphia, 1960. The text has been frequently reprinted and is available in a paperback edition, Pan Books, in association with Heinemann, London, 1970, also reprinted many times.

Background reading

CUNLIFFE, M. (ED.): *American Literature since 1900*, Sphere Books, London, 1975. For a general background to modern American literature.

HASSAN, I.: *Contemporary American Literature 1945–1972: an Introduction*, Ungar, New York, 1973. For a general background to modern American literature.

RUBIN, L. D., JNR: *The Faraway Country: Writers of the Modern South*, University of Washington Press, Seattle, 1963. For a specific account of the literature of the American South.

McCULLERS, C.: *The Heart is a Lonely Hunter*, Penguin Books, Harmondsworth, 1961.

McCULLERS, C.: *The Member of the Wedding*, Penguin Books, Harmondsworth, 1962. Both books by McCullers may be used for comparative purposes, while considering other Southern novelists working on similar themes.

The author of these notes

ROSAMUND METCALF, MA, B LITT, was educated at the University of Oxford. From 1965 until her marriage to a United Nations official in 1971 she was a lecturer in English Literature at Manchester University. Since then she was lectured at Chulalongkorn University, Bangkok, Thailand, and at Fourah Bay College, University of Sierra Leone, West Africa. She is now a lecturer in English at the University of Swaziland.

The first 250 titles